T0319018

Cambridge Elements ≡

Elements in Histories of Emotions and the Senses
edited by
Rob Boddice
Tampere University
Piroska Nagy
Université du Québec à Montréal (UQAM)
Mark Smith
University of South Carolina

MEMES, HISTORY AND EMOTIONAL LIFE

Katie Barclay
University of Adelaide
Leanne Downing
University of New South Wales

CAMBRIDGE
UNIVERSITY PRESS

CAMBRIDGE
UNIVERSITY PRESS

Shaftesbury Road, Cambridge CB2 8EA, United Kingdom

One Liberty Plaza, 20th Floor, New York, NY 10006, USA

477 Williamstown Road, Port Melbourne, VIC 3207, Australia

314–321, 3rd Floor, Plot 3, Splendor Forum, Jasola District Centre,
New Delhi – 110025, India

103 Penang Road, #05–06/07, Visioncrest Commercial, Singapore 238467

Cambridge University Press is part of Cambridge University Press & Assessment,
a department of the University of Cambridge.

We share the University's mission to contribute to society through the pursuit of
education, learning and research at the highest international levels of excellence.

www.cambridge.org
Information on this title: www.cambridge.org/9781009073295

DOI: 10.1017/9781009063715

First published 2023

A catalogue record for this publication is available from the British Library.

ISBN 978-1-009-07329-5 Paperback
ISSN 2632-1068 (online)
ISSN 2632-105X (print)

Memes, History and Emotional Life

Elements in Histories of Emotions and the Senses

DOI: 10.1017/9781009063715
First published online: June 2023

Katie Barclay
University of Adelaide

Leanne Downing
University of New South Wales

Author for correspondence: Katie Barclay, katie.barclay@adelaide.edu.au

Abstract: Internet memes are recognised for their role in creating community through shared humour or in-group cultural knowledge. One category of meme uses historical art pieces, coupled with short texts or dialogue, as a form of social commentary on both past and present. These memes often rely on a (mis)reading of the emotions of those represented in such artwork for humorous purposes. As such, they provide an important example of transhistorical engagement between contemporary society and past artefacts centred on the nature of emotion. This Element explores the historical art meme as a key cultural form that offers insight into contemporary online emotional cultures and the ways that historical emotions enable and inform the practices of such culture. It particularly attends to humour as a mode which helps to mediate the disjuncture between past and present emotion and which enables historical emotion to 'do' political and community-building work amongst meme users.

Keywords: memes, art history, face, emotions, media

ISBNs: 9781009073295 (PB), 9781009063715 (OC)
ISSNs: 2632-1068 (online), 2632-105X (print)

Contents

1 Introduction

Painted between 1843 and 1845, Gustave Courbet's famously overwrought *Self-Portrait as The Desperate Man* (1843–1845) is a work that was likely never intended for the open market and remained in the artist's studio until his death in 1877. Featuring a wide-eyed and tormented twenty-four-year-old Courbet, this painting is commonly read by art historians as an 'expressive head' – an artistic exercise completed in the tradition of French artist Charles Le Brun (1619–1690). In the modestly sized painting (just 45 × 55 cm), the artist stares wild-eyed at the viewer. His hands tear at his shoulder-length, unkempt hair and his white shirt billows under a blue painter's smock. Painted at a time when Courbet had experienced several rejections by the Paris Salon (considered by many to be the greatest annual art exhibition in the Western world at the time), the self-portrait depicts Courbet as the quintessential tortured artist – a man who suffered for his art and was becoming disillusioned with his youthful Romantic ideals. When asked in older age to reflect on his early struggles, Courbet would later comment, 'How I was made to suffer despair in my youth!' (The Met Museum Gustave Courbet Exhibition, 27 February–18 May 2008).[1]

Fast-forward to the onset of the Covid-19 pandemic in May 2020, and a digitised image of Courbet's self-portrait finds itself shared as an image macro meme on the Facebook page of the Department of History at Florida State University. This time, instead of representing Courbet as a tortured artist in a moment of existential crisis, Courbet's face is used as an emotional proxy for the face of every university student who attempts to log in to a Zoom session only to anxiously discover that they are twenty minutes late. As a digital media artefact shared by an academic institution, *The Desperate Man* meme serves as humorous and cautionary commentary on the emotions of being late for an online meeting or class. The audience, in this case, university-level history students and academics, are likely to understand the inherent humour of mixing this text with this particular artistic reference, yet it barely matters if they don't; Courbet's face does the emotional work and messaging for them. In his wide eyes and flared nostrils, students and staff are expected to recognise a sensation of something like alarm and distress, and can readily transplant those feelings onto their own experiences of running late for an online class or meeting. The meme, therefore, serves as both a humorous in-joke for a specific group of people, and a warning about the unnecessary stress that running late will engender. For a brief moment, the intended recipients of this meme are asked not simply to 'identify with' Courbet's emotion, but rather to *become* the meme and take on Courbet's emotion as if it were their own.

---

[1] www.metmuseum.org/exhibitions/listings/2008/gustave-courbet/photo-gallery)

Figure 1 'When you realize your zoom session started meme', *Department of History, Florida State University Facebook Page*, 20 May 2020.[2]

Several important questions arise as we reflect on the historical art memes' appropriation of historical emotions. What does it mean to use the facial expressions and emotions of historical agents as a stand-in for contemporary emotional experiences? In what ways do historical art meme makers usurp and rework historical emotions to express digital selves? What is the significance of the emoting historical face in these memes? And which emotions are most commonly expressed in this unique meme sub-genre? As we discuss in this Element, *The Desperate Man* meme is just one of many that use either exaggerated or impassive facial expressions from historical art works as a way of articulating contemporary emotional experiences. In some cases, the emotions expressed in these memes are consistent with those intended by the original artist, while at other times, the emotions are misread or consciously reinterpreted to create new, ironic or self-reflective statements about human emotional experience in digital culture. In most of the examples, however, the locus of the historical emotion is reflected away from the individuals depicted in the original artwork and appropriated by the individuals who create and/or share the meme across various digital platforms. The creators and recipients of historical art memes deploy historical emotion as a form of self-expression. Put simply, historical

---

[2] www.facebook.com/139850989436/photos/meme-tuesday-when-you-realize-your-zoom-ses sion-started-20-min-ago-meme-credit-l/10158308585264437/

art memes are used as a mask in a performance of an emotional self, often to convey emotions that are contested, uncomfortable or difficult to express or in situations of novelty or confusion, like the expectations for pandemic living in the digital age.

In this Element, we explore the intersection of contemporary emotional expression and historical art through the lens of digital media studies and histories of emotion. We reflect on how emotions are lived, performed and (re)negotiated across time and place and consider how groups of people who share specific temporal, demographic, psychographic or algorithmic common-alities find a sense of community, belonging and self-expression within the historical art meme. Understanding the interplay between art history, emotions and digital culture necessitates a convergence of theoretical approaches. As such, this Element draws on relevant scholarship produced within the fields of communications and digital media theory, the history of emotions, art history, and feminist new materialism. When deployed together, these approaches provide insight into how we understand, communicate and share emotions across time and place. Specifically, in applying the 'more than human' philo-sophical approaches of feminist new materialist scholars such as Barad (2003, 2007), Haraway (2003) and Braidotti (2019), the ways in which emotion-based meanings and understandings are perpetually configured and reconfigured through assemblages of human and non-human interaction can be articulated.

This work particularly considers how these (re)assemblages of emotion occur over time and place. We extend Rosenwein's (2015) concept of 'generations', where historical emotions are redeployed by later generations for new purposes, to highlight the intentionality and playfulness that can be inherent in such new configurations of historical feeling. This work therefore contributes to a scholarship that seeks to understand the nature and basis of transhistorical emotions (e.g. D'Arcens, 2014; D'Arcens & Lynch, 2018), furthering our understanding of the relationship between historical and contemporary emo-tional life and the way that modern publics engage with the past. It also contributes to meme scholarship by considering how the historical art meme uses the faces and gestures of historical actors as a way to explore, express and perform feelings that are often difficult to express in contemporary digital culture. Given the limited space, this Element concentrates on exploring the theoretical and conceptual issues that help us interpret the efficacy of the historical art meme, providing a framework for future empirical analysis.

Historical Art Memes

Discussions around memes as forms of emotional performance have peppered academic literature over the past decade (Bristow & Bown, 2019; Gal, Shifman,

& Kampf, 2016; Miltner, 2014; Nissenbaum & Shifman, 2015; Silvestri, 2018). However, to date, little sustained academic research has been conducted on the historical art meme. In seeking to address this gap, this Element explores the complexities of how specific historical depictions of emotion are (re)interpreted, expressed, coded, datafied, dispersed, and re-imagined across digital media platforms. It considers the layering of emotional expressions and cultural politics that are present within such memes and asks how we understand, share, embody and utilise these emotions in our current historical moment. This Element explores what historical art memes tell us about how we currently read and communicate emotion, our desire to connect and identify with these emoting bodies and faces, and why historical artistic representations of emotion are so useful as social commentary.

Contemporary internet memes, commonly referred to just as 'memes', are sharable links or files that are rapidly spread via digital networks and social media platforms (Shifman, 2014). One of the most common forms of memes, and the type that we will discuss throughout this Element, is the image macro meme, a piece of digital media that typically features a photo or artwork with text superimposed over the image. The text of an image macro meme usually contains a witty and/or satirical message, which works playfully with the image being used. Today, image macro memes are a central part of participatory digital culture and play a key role in user experiences of online networks such as 4chan, Quora, and Reddit, as well as social media platforms such as Twitter, Facebook, Tik-Tok, and Instagram. In their totality, these digital media networks combine with easy-to-use image editing software to enable individuals to share their feelings about a wide range of popular issues to large audiences at a rapid pace.

As digital media artefacts, internet memes are powerful conduits of emotion. Easily produced and quickly disseminated by the real-time affordances of digital and social media platforms, memes function as accessible and rapidly reproducible forms of vernacular communication, through which the frustrations, triumphs, joys, and power struggles of everyday life can be easily shared and expressed. From gender roles, relationships, and sex, through to workplace cultures, technology usage, and food consumption, memes have the power to connect and conflate the minutia of personal experience with a seemingly endless array of macro-level social, cultural, and political phenomena.

Most commonly characterised by their transient, irreverent and often perverse humour, memes are far more than fleeting internet jokes shared by like-minded individuals. Instead, they exist as unique cultural units, capable of conveying important insights into how individuals and communities emotionally 'manage' the present (Silvestri, 2018). Indeed, as is increasingly acknowledged within contemporary scholarship on the topic, memes themselves exist not simply because they are 'funny' and easy to spread, but because humans have emotional investments in them. As Milner and Phillips (2017) argue, people save, share, and remix cultural units not solely for play but also from a sense of anger, fear, or confusion. Memes provide space to express and perform emotion in relation to a changing environment.

While internet memes are by nature ephemeral, certain types of memes have managed to achieve a type of 'sticking power' that enables them to stay culturally relevant over a number of years. One such genre is the historical art meme: a unique amalgam of art history, political commentary and dark humour that is characterised by a juxtaposition between fine arts and present-day participatory culture. These memes typically use art styles that provide access to the expression and performance of emotion, with a particular focus on emotion as expressed through faces, gestures, and bodies. From the tense and extravagant works of Rubens and Caravaggio through to the dramatic portraiture of Rembrandt, Vermeer, and Woltze, historical art memes are ripe with an aesthetics of fear, despair, anger, sadness, love, lust, piety, and boredom.

In their totality, art-history memes occupy significant digital real estate. They frequently appear in online magazines such as Bored Panda and Art Space, and on media aggregation sites such as Reddit. Social media platforms such as Twitter, Instagram, Pinterest, and Facebook are also regular points of dissemination, with one particularly popular historical art memes Facebook page currently attracting well over 5 million followers (Classical Art Memes,)[3] all of whom are likely to have their own assortment of political, social, religious, and demographic realities. While some of the memes that we have used in this Element are shared by identifiable sources with predictable audiences (such as the University of Florida History Department), most have surfaced in disparate corners of the internet and are replicated widely, making it difficult to pinpoint the precise creator and their intended audience. As a result, we can only make a series of educated assumptions about the creators and 'audiences' of our chosen memes.

As Wiggins (2019) has argued, defining the exact audience of a meme isn't always an easy task. It is often not possible to detail specific audiences and modes of reception in digital media, largely because online media does not usually follow the same 'top-down' producer-receiver approach that once existed for traditional media sources such as letters, manuscripts, newspapers, radio, or television. Where scholars of non-digital media can often specify the intention, dissemination, and reception of media texts, the reception and production of memes is far more diffuse and volatile. Memes are by their very nature polysemic and instantly transformable – they can be taken up and interpreted in a wide variety of ways by a diverse assortment of people, and

---

[3] www.facebook.com/classicalartmemes/?ref=page_internal

in some instances, a single meme can receive several vastly different receptions depending on where or when it is shared. Following Wiggins, we therefore recognise that when it comes to understanding memes, we are at best only able to discuss what he terms as an 'imagined audience' – one which is addressed through various forms of digital and social media, and one which is constituted by a mix of both 'real' and hypothetical individuals, and their perceived desires, whims, and proclivities.

As aggregate digital artefacts of the twenty-first century, memes are collectively created, circulated and transformed by large numbers of participants across diverse social networks. Fuelled by the velocity of digital media platforms, memes allow individuals to make far-reaching social connections and become active agents in the creation of public conversations and cultural debates. In observing the participatory nature of this phenomena, several meme scholars have drawn attention to the ways in which memes help to form and signify communal belonging (Jenkins, Ito, & boyd, 2015; Moreno-Almeida, 2020; Nissenbaum & Shifman, 2015). In particular, Limor Shifman (2014) has referred to the proliferation of memes in digital culture as being akin to a type of postmodern folklore, in which social norms and values are created through shared cultural objects and come to shape and reflect larger social mindsets. Following Shifman, Milner (2016) has noted that memes allow small, individual strands of commentary to be woven together into larger, vibrant cultural tapestries and media ecologies.

The capacity of memes to shape and reflect social sentiments has led to a considerable amount of academic attention. Notably, scholars in the fields of communication and digital media have had much to say about the ways in which memes invoke a sense of belonging (Milner, 2016), demonstrate cultural capital (Nissenbaum & Shifman, 2015), and construct collective identities (Miltner, 2014; Nagle, 2017). A shared touchstone of many of these explorations is the work of Pierre Bourdieu (1986), whose concepts of cultural capital and habitus have led to rich conversations around the ways in which the popularity of memes relies upon their ability to demonstrate familiarity with a particular culture's symbols, nomenclature, and social norms (DeCook, 2018; Ignatow & Robinson, 2017).

This Element gives particular attention to historical art memes that act as a social commentary on gender relationships or feminist politics, a popular form of historical art meme that provides some boundaries on a large field of evidence. Given that creating or sharing a meme implies a belief that the sentiment or world view expressed within it will resonate with others, we are able to identify a series of social, psychographic, and demographic commonalities that the creators and imagined audiences of our chosen memes are likely to share. These commonalities are as follows. Most of the memes presented in this Element likely favour an educated audience who are both internet savvy *and* to some degree interested in art history. Many of the text-based jokes and juxta-positions used within our selected historical art memes show a leaning towards progressive, feminist-inspired politics, and commonly use 'dark humour' and satire as a way of expressing personal emotions around social issues such as gendered power relations, female sexual frustration, sexual harassment, and/or mansplaining. The selected memes that do not include a feminist message of this kind tend to focus on the emotional sensitivities of men as they perform themselves online – specifically, how the (assumed male) meme creators felt about being shocked, late, shamed, or ridiculed in an online or digital setting. It is worth noting here that in all of the 'non-feminist' examples we selected, the central visual motif seems to be about a 'feminised' vulnerability that men profess to feel about performing themselves and their gender identities online. Specifically, visual attention is drawn to open and/or leaking facial orifices, wide eyes, or absurd representations of femininity that come to stand in for the men who create the memes. Across all of these memes is a concern with gender presentation and power relationships that is suggestive of the anxieties of the culture under study. If this is only one possible reading of the material, the larger principles of how historical art memes come to be deployed as part of contem-porary emotional expression have wider application.

The use of dark humour is a common thread throughout nearly all of the memes that we have selected for this Element. This is representative of the type of humour that appears in the historical art memes in our research. It is also consistent with what Silvestri (2021) has identified as 'internet gallows humour'. Silvestri (2021) makes the argument that many of today's internet memes showcase the emergence of a 'gallows humour' that is common among millennials who identify with a certain upwardly mobile class, and possess an adequate level of education, financial independence and social capital. She notes that this 'audience' relies on 'relatively new technological affordances to create and circulate meaning' amongst themselves. Many of the memes selected for this Element reflect the humour and world view of the demographic outlined by Silvestri. However, where Silvestri investigates gallows humour via a selection of 'nihilist' memes which show a lessening of attachment to the promise of a 'good life', the memes selected for this volume do something different. They evidence not so much a letting-go of the cruel optimism of an impossible 'dream', but rather an expression of struggle, emergence, and frustration over issues such as social power, bodily autonomy, and the online self. To this end, we argue that many historical art memes actively express emotions that are otherwise hard to articulate within digital culture.

Doing Emotion with Memes

Community building and belonging are emotional processes, yet how memes 'do' emotion is still underexplored, as is their role as emotional artefacts that operate within today's commercialised and datafied media environments. The role of emotion in enabling digital media to function, including its role in the operation of big data collection, algorithms, and monetisation, is yet to be given sustained attention. Within communication and digital media scholarship for example, many contemporary discussions about memes have tended to bypass conversations about the social and temporal relationality of emotions in favour of the political, technological, and sociological throughputs of those emotions. Thus, while an abundance of meme research now focusses on the capacity of memes to bring people together (Merrill & Lindgren, 2021), make money (Williams, 2000), influence politics (Chagas et al., 2019), and mobilise grass-root political protests (Makhortykh & González Aguilar, 2020), much less attention has been devoted to understanding how emotions in and of themselves are understood, (re)produced, and refracted across digital media landscapes. This observation is in keeping with a larger point made by Ellis and Tucker (2020), who note that while understanding emotions in social media is a developing field, a sustained consideration of how emotions are inevitably relational, situational, and socially produced is lacking.

Analysing digital media artefacts through the lens of historically and socially situated emotions is yet to be fully explored in contemporary scholarship. Indeed, future studies into memes will likely be enhanced by the work of affect and emotion scholars who repeatedly demonstrate that reading and interpreting emotions in cultural texts requires a robust understanding of how emotions themselves are socially contextualised, received and (re)produced across time and place (Ahmed, 2014; Barclay, 2020; D'Arcens, 2014). The efficacy of such readings is perhaps exemplified in the historical art meme, which places historical emotion – in the form of a historical artwork – at the centre of contemporary emotional practices.

Far from being human universals, emotions – as well as their expression and representation, not least on the body itself – are shaped by culture and society (Barclay, 2020; Boddice, 2018; Plamper, 2015). The naming of an emotion, its characteristics, valence (whether we view it positively or negatively), and how it should be felt and expressed vary. Significantly, cultural norms for emotional life are not simply an overlay on a shared biology, but actively enable the embodied experience of feeling, how it is interpreted, and what actions should arise from an emotional experience. Not all emotions exist in all times and places, and the emotional repertoire available to individuals shapes their feelings and emotional expression. People are educated in the display of emotion on the body, and in how to represent that in art and writing, which in turn shapes how emotions are understood across generations and how historians access past emotion. Historical sources, like artworks, are not emotions, but as well as giving insight into how a culture understands emotion, they – like memes today – could be deployed as part of emotional practices or performances. The early modern love letter not only shared an expression of love between writer and recipient, but acted as an emotional object that could be used, among other things, as a memory aid, a contract, and physical evidence of the intangible (Barnes, 2017). Through emotional practices such as this, people give expression and shape to embodied feelings and extend them to produce emotional communities (Rosenwein, 2011).

Historical sources must be deployed carefully as evidence of emotional life. Each source – a letter, a novel, a painting – is informed by genre rules that set expectations for its form. Emotions expressed in historical sources are mediated through these cultural rules and an understanding of form is required to interpret the expression and functions of emotion within different cultures. Contemporary interpretations are significant too. Historians' understanding of the past and past feelings is rapidly expanding, and as they do, how we interpret past source materials evolves. Thus, historical emotion is multiply mediated, not only through the source materials that give it shape but contemporary knowledges and interpretative frameworks. Many engagements with the historical art meme, often intentionally, ignore the contexts of their production and how these originally shaped the emotions on display. Indeed, the humour of many historical art memes arises from an awareness that contemporary uses of such imagery rely on 'misreadings' of historical emotion displays, and so consideration of the historicity of emotion is critical to the efficacy of the meme. This Element unpacks the layers of emotional expression evident in historical art memes and considers them within the social contexts of the original artwork as well as their present-day usage. Throughout emotions are treated not as 'fixed' or innate biological entities but as cultural products. As such, this Element highlights the intersections between the ways emotions are understood and practiced and how different societies operate and are organised.

Memes, History and Emotional Life

This Element is designed to provide readers with the tools to understand how the historical art meme works to produce a transhistorical emotional engagement, and how that engagement in turn becomes an effective mode of emotional performance in the digital world. Early sections offer an account of the theoretical and conceptual frameworks from digital media studies and the history of emotions that are brought together in this volume to explain the phenomenon of the historical art meme. Cognisant that this is an interdisciplinary project, sections 2 and 3 outline the key insights of the fields combined here that help us understand the operation of emotion across time and in the digital environment. Section 4 attends to historical art as a source of emotion, seeking to 'denaturalize' the portrait and provide some basic insights into the generic rules that shape how emotions are expressed in this form. This was felt to be important as the humour of the historical art meme often revolves around the disjuncture between the seeming 'realism' of the face or body on display and its redeployment in 'unnatural' ways, that disrupt or at least put into question our capacity to interpret historical emotion.

Later sections apply the ideas discussed in earlier sections to two case studies of historical art memes that provide social commentary on gender and feminist politics and which use art works originally produced in Europe from the seventeenth to nineteenth centuries. Gender politics is a core theme of the historical art meme genre and the examples selected here are popular and widely disseminated. The period when the original art was made – where portraiture and conversation pieces offer numerous examples of delicately rendered emotions – offers a rich array of material for meme users and so reflects a considerable share of the works used in the historical art meme genre. These constraints are used here to offer some parameters for discussion, but the wider principles of how historical art memes are deployed to enable contemporary emotional practices applies to the genre more widely.

This Element considers the historical art meme as a complex digital media phenomenon in which past and present emotions are profoundly interconnected yet strangely disjointed. As a product of an always-on, always-active, always-monetised digital media environment, historical art memes demonstrate not only how emotions reverberate and morph through time and space, but how they are appropriated as modern-day technologies of the self.

2 How Memes Do Emotion

When Florida State University's History Department circulated Courbet's portrait as a commentary on the emotional experience of pandemic life, they used a historical artwork to express emotion and to create a community around that shared emotional experience. This process was enabled by several factors, including the semantic richness of the meme, which allowed it to convey a relatively complex message, the emotions that its audience associated with such symbolism, and the capacity for shared emotion to promote community and belonging. An important dimension of its efficacy was its playful character. The meme offered a series of comedic juxtapositions – past and present emotions, familiarity and strangeness, despair and humour – that encouraged the audience to enter into the emotional experience being offered by the poster. Humour was deployed not only for its own sake, but to further a richer and more complex set of feelings. The capacity of different media to enable emotional communities is now well studied, but the efficacy of the meme, and the type of communities it produces, are also informed by the nature of the digital environment in which they are shared. This section introduces the conceptual and theoretical background that invites this reading of the Courbet meme, particularly attending to the importance of the digital environment in shaping the operation of the meme, the use of symbolism to enable emotional communities, and the role of humour as a mediator of emotional experience. While this Element concerns itself with the historical art meme, much of the discussion in this section pertains to the meme genre in general.

Memes, Symbolism, and Emotions

The Courbet meme contains a depth of meaning. It combines a historical painting, which brings its own history of making, reception, and survival over time, with contemporary commentary that references wider social, political, and environmental conditions. This is brought to the public by a content creator on a social media platform (Facebook) that itself holds an array of meanings for users and the wider public. All of these dimensions of the meme contribute to how it is interpreted by audiences and shape its capacity to communicate effectively. Central to the communication intended by the Courbet meme is an expression of emotion – the meme's audience is invited to recognise the emotional experience being conveyed and to embrace it as their own. The meme depicts emotions for consumption, invites the audience to enter into that emotion, and uses that same shared emotion to encourage engagement with the page and social media site in general. Viewers are encouraged to invest in the meme, at least to the extent that they stop scrolling and share in its communication.

Scholarly enquiry into the emotionally enabling role of cultural texts now constitutes a significant field, not least since the 'affective turn' within the humanities. Much of this work relies on the capacity of the 'symbol' to carry a multiplicity of meanings that a knowing audience can interpret and to which they respond. Here emotion is not reduced simply to personal feelings or psychological states, but rather is recognised as a diverse cultural practice that is given meaning through its relationship with bodies, politics, and social alliances, and which comes into being through its circulation between actors (Ott, 2017). The capacity of symbols to enable the practice of emotion has particularly been explored by Ahmed (2014) and Berlant (2008), who each highlight how texts are infused with emotion and subsequently come to shape wider society and various forms of power relations. Ahmed (2014), in particular, has suggested that emotions come to circulate as people and things become 'sticky' with emotion as a result of histories of contact between socially and politically situated bodies, objects, and signs. Hate, for example, 'sticks' to groups of people, such as refugees, because of how they are represented, and this in turn informs how they are treated by those that encounter them. In a similar way, memes become 'sticky' with emotion as they mobilise symbols and ideas familiar to their audience. This, in turn, enables them to create communities as they circulate.

As intra-cultural texts that routinely juxtapose ideas or iconography from diverse places, memes have the capacity to combine a broad array of ideas and to be especially potent vehicles for enabling the emotions that 'stick' to them. Many memes, including those that we discuss in the following sections, are imbued with multiple layers of meaning, with each new adaptation of a meme purposefully building on the ones that came before. One version of the widely memed portrait of Joseph Ducreux displaying a mocking expression (*Portrait de l'artiste sous les traits d'un moqueur*, 1793), for example, is overlaid with the text 'Gentlemen, I inquire who hath released the hounds?', an 'archaic' translation of a lyric from the song 'Who Let the Dog's Out?' (Figure 2). The latter song was a critical commentary on 'bro-culture' and the sexual harassment of women by men (the 'dogs' who couldn't control themselves) (Raivio, 2016). The humour of the meme lies in interpreting Ducreux's facial expression and bodily gestures as that of a 'bro' and aligning this behaviour with men over generations. It is a reading that requires knowledge of 'bro culture' and its embodied expression, of feminist critiques of such culture, of the song, of 'archaic' text speak, where modern references are imagined into a pseudo-historical expression, and of art history, at least to the extent that this portrait is recognised as a historical work redeployed for a new purpose. As each layer brings its own emotional connotations and resonances, the potential of the meme to engage its audience and invite an emotional response is enhanced. As this example suggests, memes function not simply through an advanced form of cultural literacy (Knobel & Lankshear, 2014), but also *emotional literacy*, relying on the ability of the viewer to translate the significance of the text's intertwining layers and recognise its humorous potential. Following Milner's (2016) work on memes and participation, this emotional literacy can

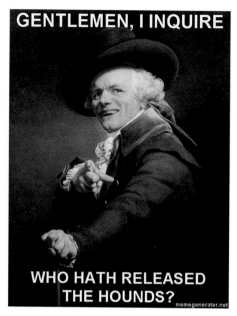

Figure 2 'Who Let the Dogs Out Ducreux Meme', *Know Your Meme*, 18 February 2021, https://knowyourmeme.com/photos/1971671-who-let-the-dogs-out

be identified as a type of cultural gatekeeping, which effectively marks the boundaries between being 'in the know' and being outside of the group, and so produces the limits of the emotional community and who 'belongs'.

Memes speak to an 'in-crowd' and tap into jokes or sentiments that draw explicitly from pre-existing cultural knowledge banks and obscure cultural references. In perpetually remixing, parodying and re-appropriating popular texts and images, memes create a mode of sticky signification and emotional participation that is always, inevitably, more diffuse than the meme itself. To suggest that 'belonging' is an important part of meme culture is to recognise that belonging comes with a set of culturally specific emotional rules, rituals, and repertoires that must not only be intellectually understood but also symbolically represented. One way that many memes achieve this is through the use of a shared, common language. As McCulloch (2019) has pointed out, memes utilise a series of distinct language patterns and repeated phrases as a way of encouraging people with similar life experiences to relate to each other and reproduce further texts that talk to the particularities of those circumstances. As we explore below, this shared language extends to a collective understanding of how to interpret facial expressions and bodily gestures, which additionally function as a way of expressing and 'doing' emotion within the community.

Emotions not only 'stick' to memes, with real-world effects, but the use of memes become an opportunity to perform and collectively renegotiate emotion for new environments.

Evolving Emotional Communities

The followers of the Facebook page of the Florida State University History Department, through a shared appreciation of the Courbet meme, were encouraged to form a new emotional community, one whose feeling rules were suited to the new conditions of Zoom learning in pandemic conditions. As psychosocial entities, memes allow digital media users to bridge the gap between individual and collective emotions (Davison, 2012). Personal experiences of emotion such as sadness, love, fear, shame, and jealousy all find sympathetic (and sometimes not so sympathetic) homes in memes, as do expressions of complex individual experiences, such as depression, anxiety, and suicidality. Accordingly, scholarship is now emerging in the fields of mental health, clinical psychology and neuroscience that explore the ways emotionally vulnerable people might use memes to find emotional support, comradery, solace, and validation (Akram et al., 2021; McCosker & Gerrard, 2021; Mitra, 2020; Willenborg, 2019). Shifman (2014) argues that this complex intertwining between personal feeling and broader cultural sentiments serves as a convenient way for digital media users to 'have it all'. In observing the 'networked individualism' of contemporary internet users, she points towards the ways in which individuals upload self-made memes to signify to their peers that they are digitally literate, unique and creative, while at the same time relying on safe structures of widely shared memetic formulas and linguistic codes. Creators of memes are therefore able to simultaneously express both their uniqueness and their connectivity in relative safety (Shifman, 2014). Notably this mirrors how people communicate emotion more generally, where personal feelings are given expression and cultural significance through shared norms of emotional expression and performance.

Emotions are given form and meaning through their articulation using a shared language and normative rules for feeling. Rosenwein (2011) suggests that groups that are defined through their shared expression and valuation of emotion (whether a feeling is 'good' or 'bad') can be understood as emotional communities, groups that overlap with social communities. Here emotions are not 'natural' or 'universal' biological experiences that groups share with each other to create community, but rather community is enabled through their group production of emotion and emotion rules. Understood through this framework, memes can be viewed not simply as expressive of emotions that pre-exist in a surrounding culture, but as locations where new emotions and emotional practices can be realised. Meme users often rely on broader cultural understandings and expression of emotion, as well as the emotional meanings associated with the content of their memes, in order to make connections with like-feeling others. Yet, as sites where communities explore, contest and collaborate about and with emotion, memes are also opportunities to rebuild and reform feeling rules. Thus, the meme community becomes implicated in hierarchies of power that are supported through conforming with or resisting normative emotional practices.

The anthropologist and historian William Reddy (2001) suggests that emotional norms can act to enforce 'emotional regimes', where those who fail to conform to expectations for feeling can find their ability to exercise power limited or even removed. Within cultures with little space for emotional liberty, like-feeling communities can find each other in 'emotional refuges', where they are provided space to redefine emotion and emotional practices for their own community. A well-studied example of the emotional refuge is the space created by gay subcultures in contexts where homosexual practices were subversive (Meek, 2017). By providing outlets for those who suffered under dominant emotional rules, gay subcultures not only experienced emotional relief but created a new emotional culture that came to challenge and ultimately subvert normative heterosexual expectations for feeling. The dialogic relationship between dominant and subculture expressions of emotion enabled an evolution in ideas and expectations for emotional life. In a similar manner, meme culture, not least through its continual remixing and reformulating of expectations, provides a site to contest and evolve feeling. As Reckwitz (2012) suggests, the continual refiguration of ideas, bodies and objects not only allows affective spaces to materialise but provides opportunities for their transformation. Returning to Ahmed's concept of 'stickiness', where meaning and so relations of power, are produced through the saturation of symbols with ideas and feelings, the continual evolution of the meme form allows old and new meanings and emotions to realign, and sometimes dissolve, with use and reuse. The Courbet meme that offers old feelings for a new experience – the Zoom classroom – provides an opportunity to explore the appropriate feeling rules for a rapidly changing, and increasingly digital, world.

Online Emotions

The meme offers a text that supports the production of an emotional community, but its capacity to do so is in no small part due to its placement within a digital environment that allows for its rapid spread and evolution. Part of the meme's efficacy for emotional life reflects the central role that emotion plays within the digital domain. There has been significant scholarly commentary around the relationship between individuals and the datafied practices of tracking, measuring and monetising emotions online (Ellis & Tucker, 2020; Tettegah, 2016). Today, data generated by tracking bodily and emotional practices informs many commercial interests and industries. Digital media advertising, in particular, is well known for its use of sophisticated algorithms to map and predict individual users' emotional states and viewing/buying habits based on age, gender, place, and previous social media 'likes'. This datafication of the human experience situates memes and meme culture within a unique climate of emotional expression and sociality – one that is not simply created through a gathering of like-minded people in politically and economically neutral spaces or commons, but rather one that is only made visible through the processes and filters of monetised digital media platforms (Fuchs, 2014; Nash, 2016; Zuboff, 2019). The emotional community being built through Courbet's meme is given form through the algorithmic rhythms of Facebook and the economic interests that underpin its operation.

A good example of the datafied context of emotional expression in the digital age is the popular social news aggregate service, Reddit, which is used extensively by meme creators and their audiences. Reddit has recently achieved a market value of US $10 billion, and it has done so by strategically selling its audience's emotional data (Isaac, 2021). As a platform that promotes itself as a 'network of communities where people can dive into their interests, hobbies and passions', Reddit encourages its 52 million active daily users to 'up-vote' or 'down-vote' content generated by its audience. It then sells advertising space to organisations that want to reach specific parts of that audience. By tracking its users' emotional, social, and political expressions, Reddit effectively turns emotional expressions and preferences into monetised data. It then hedges its bets and offers a premium subscription service where members who are tired of being advertised to can pay to enjoy an 'ad-free' experience.

This datafication of online emotional expressions has led to a complex situation in which individual users are encouraged to look 'inwards' in order to create more and more personalised and emotionally compelling content, at the same time as their information is being mined and aggregated into a depersonalised system of mass data generation. While a meme creator may feel personally empowered, validated or disappointed by the number of shares, likes or up-votes elicited by their meme, a large part of what makes a meme go 'viral', or sink into obscurity, is its capacity to tap into commercially driven social media algorithms and protocols, which are in turn fed by user emotion in the form of 'likes' or 'votes'.

This intertwining of the emotional, subjective individual with digital communication and data aggregation technologies offers a pertinent reminder that in today's digitally networked society, digital technology can no longer be talked about as if it were in some way separate from or an extension of our individual identities. Indeed, as many scholars, including Robert Cover (2015) and Deborah Lupton (2018), have argued, our lives are now so entangled with the digital that there is no longer any real sense of being online or offline; there is just life in the digital. The memes produced in online spaces should not be considered at one step of remove from individual feeling or social life, but rather a key site where emotion is performed and negotiated, both by individuals and collectives. As a result, the emotional community that is built through meme culture is actively shaped by datification practices, where audiences for memes are produced through their previous preferences and perceived openness to particular forms of marketing. Within this context, datafication practices underpin the form of the meme genre, reinforcing particular modes of expression or 'feeling rules' as effective for community building and weeding out alternatives. Here the boundaries of community are less defined by geography or demographics than by members' emotional responsiveness to particular media; the emotional community is given shape around its online content and its capacity to serve market interests. Part of what enables the efficacy of the contemporary meme in the digital sphere is humour, an emotional experience that has long been associated with both the subversion and consolidation of power (Barclay, 2019a).

Humour as a Site of Societal Opportunity

The picture of Courbet overset with the words 'When you realize your zoom session started 20 minutes ago' can be described as humorous, where the humour arises from the clever juxtaposition of an expressive face from a pre-digital age offset by an online experience. The audience recognises that Courbet's expression could not be caused by Zoom due to the dating of the painting, but nonetheless are willing to recognise a shared, familiar, and transhistorical emotion between Courbet and themselves. This contradiction – emotion that is both distant and strange, but familiar and useful to interpreting present experience – places the Courbet meme as a site of a humour and one that allows the reader to reflect on the appropriate emotions for the new Zoom world in which they live. Humour plays an integral role in meme culture; however, not all memes are light-hearted or unsophisticated (Beer, 2013). Using wit, sarcasm, humour, and ridicule, many memes weigh in on hefty issues such as politics (DeCook, 2018), health (MacDonald, 2021), race (Al-Natour, 2020), and gender (Miltner, 2014).

Recent studies into the use of memes during times of crisis or social upheaval, for example, have observed a tendency to satirise significant events and use laughter as a means of collective coping (Flecha et al., 2020; Tandoc & Takahashi, 2016). As Silvestri (2018) observes, memes convey important insights into how communities and individuals emotionally 'manage' the present.

A significant body of work is already devoted to the role that humour plays in maintaining social and community boundaries. Kessel and Merziger (2012), for example, highlight the ways in which humour was used as a device throughout the twentieth century to effectively negotiate belonging and mark the boundaries of inclusion and exclusion, which commonly ran along predictable lines of race, class, sexuality, and gender. Similarly, Bremmer and Roodenburg (1997) and Cheauré and Nohejl (2014) demonstrate how humour has been used as a way of coping and maintaining order during times of social friction and confusion. Recent scholarship on twenty-first century internet memes reflects the above findings. Harlow, Rowlett, & Huse (2020), Sover (2018), and Penney (2020) argue that while humorous memes show great potential for creating alternative public spheres for marginalised voices, they commonly maintain existing social power structures. Thus, while it is tempting to celebrate humorous memes for their ability to bring minority groups together in moments of collective laughter, it is also prudent to reflect upon the ways in which humour is also used to manage and maintain the status quo.

Billig (2005) contends that while laughter and humour have always been important parts of daily life, it is often the darker practices of ridicule and shaming that reinforce social power dynamics. While observing that humour can be rebellious and actively kick against the dictates of social life, Billig also makes it clear that ridicule plays a distinctly disciplinary function and ensures that members of society routinely comply with the customs and habits of their social milieu. If laughter in the form of ridicule and mockery is central to social life, so too is it essential in the creation, deployment, and reception of contemporary internet memes. Indeed, like a diverse range of humorous texts throughout history, memes that deliberately mock, debase, or transgress cultural norms ultimately provide a rich commentary on our concerns and limitations. Memes identify and historically contextualise collectively held anxieties around issues such as social change, cultural tolerance and religious or social structures.

If this is the case, opportunities or sites for humour often operate as liminal spaces, offering moments to explore, contest and affirm social order. While largely absent in scholarly discussions of memes, the concept of liminality offers insight into how humour is deployed within contemporary meme culture. Turner (1979) and Campbell (2000) argue that the interplay of liminal and ludic states are central to the creation of textual, emotional and symbolic representation across a multitude of cultures. In functioning as a state of 'being on a threshold' between 'what is' and 'what is next', liminal texts, like memes themselves, are often filled with expressions of experimentation and play. Using incongruous humour, this play often moves between the boundaries of acceptable cultural norms and towards new forms of being and understanding. Following Turner, liminality is full of potency and potentiality and can manifest as a play of words, symbols, or metaphors that pushes beyond the confines of ritual and genre, and creates a form of 'plural reflexivity', whereby a community uses acts of performativity to 'portray, understand and then act on itself' (Turner, 1979).

As liminal texts, memes offer those who are stateless, voiceless, or otherwise outside of dominant culture a way of expressing feelings of tension and unease. Moreover, the liminality of memes provides an opportunity for collective and individual moments of self-reflection and critique. Indeed, it is common for both individuals and social groups to temporarily step outside of their own social, political, and ideological frameworks to find fleeting moments of personal insight and humour in particular memes (Chonka, 2019). This multiplicity of meaning, reception, and intent within the meme has led Phillips and Milner (2017) to describe participatory internet culture as being inherently 'ambivalent' or two-sided, terms that are also associated with states of liminality and play. In pointing to how memes and similar digital media artefacts use polysemous framing to be at once antagonistic and social, creative and disruptive, humorous and barbed, Phillips and Milner identify memes as fundamentally complicating the boundaries of everyday life. Accordingly, they see the binaries of online and offline, normal and abnormal and then and now, as being perpetually merged, remixed, disseminated and rejected in the process of creating new and emergent sensibilities.

The ambivalent and playful nature of memes can also facilitate a perceived union between self and text, whereby individuals profess to not simply finding a meme funny, but rather feel that they 'are' the meme. This is likely enhanced in the digital environment where memes operate as a central mode of expression to exclusively online audiences – the meme becomes the self within the online space. The liminal and ludic are bought into full view as the boundaries between self and other, personal and social, historical meaning and contemporary agency momentarily collapse. Thus, digital media users may share a meme of a classical artwork depicting an exaggerated facial expression to denote their present-day distress over losing a smartphone or missing a flight. Phillip and Milner's (2017) observations on ambivalence also offer an important reminder that memes can show us the boundaries of those emotions we are willing to express and those we repress. Memes that construct themselves around expressions of exaggeration, excess, ambivalence, shame, parody, and debasement are on some level offering audiences a type of cathartic release from the hegemonic power structures and injustices that they are otherwise forced to live within (Grigore & Molesworth, 2018). Notably, if this is the case, such ambivalences – which are prominent across meme forms – are not demoted by the digital algorithms that might be imagined as the 'rules' of social media culture, but rather provide a space for engagement that reflects their popularity and value for contemporary users and is suggestive that normative power structures take a different form in online environments.

Memes use humour to create liminal spaces, where contemporary ideas and meanings can be explored and contested. The use, expression, and display of emotion in response to novel phenomena – like a Zoom meeting – are just one of the areas that memes explore, but emotion takes on particular significance in a digital environment in which algorithms and operation are driven by the emotional expressions and engagements of its users. The emotional communities that are established around such liminal sites are defined not just by an agreement of how emotion should be expressed and valued in their culture, but by their desire to renegotiate such emotion for a rapidly evolving digital world. Within this context, historical emotions – provided to modern audiences in the form of historical paintings – offer an emotional repertoire that can be used to both enable the liminality of a text and provide exemplars for responding to novel experiences. As will be demonstrated in the following sections, historical art memes in particular provide a unique opportunity for individuals to play with the uncomfortable emotions of the present via deliberate misreading, mocking, or celebration of the past. In doing so, historical art memes deploy representations of historical emotion to explore present social and political conditions and to build emotional communities.

3 Emotions over Time

Courbet's 'expressive head', *Self-Portrait as the Desperate Man* (1845), remains evocative across the centuries. Its title is suggestive of the emotion that he wished to convey – desperation – and historical research indicates that it was produced during a period of 'melancholy' for the artist, as he struggled to build a career. The painting is not, however, an unprecedented rendering of personal feeling, sharing several gestures with Albrecht Dürer's 1515 etching of the *Desperate Man*, another work that has been interpreted as an expression of melancholy. Courbet here reinterpreted a historic artwork as an artistic exercise, and perhaps expression of the self, and in doing so engaged with an already historical emotion and used it for contemporary purposes.

Almost 200 years later, the content administrator for the Florida State University History Department in turn redeployed the historical feeling of the *Desperate Man* for a new audience, although by this date melancholy was a 'lost' emotion. Instead, the meme creator asked their audience to identify with the emotion expressed on a face and body, a feeling that was not named but rather associated with a particular social experience – running late to an online meeting. In an era of the online meeting, where people now routinely view each other as small, portrait-size boxes, that emotion was something performed on the face and body perhaps resonated more with viewers than a definition of a feeling that was still being negotiated. Whether or not this was the case, this particular meme offered its audience a transhistorical engagement with a past, even lost, emotion, and suggested its usefulness for living in the modern world.

Much of the historiography of emotions has focused on the feelings of past actors, acknowledging how the specific cultural and temporal conditions that produce emotion shape their style, expression and the political work they do for social groups. Historical emotions, however, do not stay in the past, but are communicated over time and across generations. Historical sources – whether in archival documents, books, and printed materials, in paintings or material culture – are a key mechanism through which we encounter past feelings and offer an opportunity for them to be redeployed in the present for a variety of purposes. Meme culture has embraced the representation of emotion in the past, not least through the use of paintings, drawings, and similar visual arts as foundational texts for commentary and circulation. This section explores this use of past emotion for present purposes, engaging with scholarship on trans-historical emotion, new materialism, and the ludic. It particularly interrogates how historical emotions are deployed by emotional communities to tell new histories and so generate new emotional presents and futures by meme users.

Transhistorical Emotion

All emotion is historical emotion (Barclay, 2020; Boddice, 2018; Plamper, 2015). We learn the language of emotion – to call a feeling 'love' or 'hate' – and how to express, experience, and respond to such feelings through practices of socialisation. These 'felt habits', engrained since childhood, are often natur-alised and so performed without much effort, but they can also be reformed across the life course to adjust to different expectations, or when they become unconstructive to peaceable living or flourishing (Scheer, 2012). People acquire new emotional repertoires over their lives, not least as they move into new social or economic groups with different standards for emotional behaviour. A new employee at an organisation is expected to quickly learn the emotional rules of that environment, perhaps learning to perform the polite, calm, or cheery outlook of a customer service role, or the fragile honour, and so tender feelings, of the legal world (Barclay, 2019a). Emotional rules in such contexts typically overlap with those of the wider culture in which those organisations operate but might place particular emphasis on certain forms of emotional control or expression (Hochschild, 2012a).

The emotions performed in these environments all have histories. Social and cultural norms for behaviour typically reflect the values and expectations of groups that arise from their understanding of self and identity, their role and function, and a desire to co-exist effectively within a particular context (Stearns & Stearns, 1985). These values, beliefs, and identifications are usually taught, and so rely on intergenerational knowledges (even if 'generation' here can be understood as the shallow memory of a long-standing employee versus a new hire) and a group's understanding of its own history and ways of being. Thus, a new employee might come to deploy a cheery smile not simply by mimicking those around them, but as they are taught about the history of their organisation and their core values (Hochschild, 2012a). A new entrant to a religious house might learn how to emote through engaging with the group's teachings and doctrines, desiring to align themselves with an emotional imaginary grounded in a long faith tradition (Hotchin, 2017). And Courbet might learn how to express melancholy through an encounter with a 300-year-old sketch by Dürer. Such emotional education might be explicit, through formal education, or implicit, through soft expectations and disciplines. However it is transmitted, feeling rules draw on shared histories and experiences to set norms for emotional expression and ultimately personal feeling.

This is not to suggest that there is no novelty in our emotional lives. The history of emotions shows significant variation over time and place in emotions and emotional rules, and suggests that there are a variety of mechanisms by which emotions evolve and change (Lemmings & Brooks, 2014). As a number of theorists have demonstrated, individuals who struggle to conform to or perform emotional rules can seek to resist or subvert them (Reddy, 2001). When they find 'refuge' with groups of like-feeling people they can form new emotional communities, with their own expectations and rules. Yet, new emotions are rarely entirely distinct from past feelings, and instead seek to evolve or adapt pre-existing emotional rules for new identities, experiences, or future hopes. Indeed, historical feeling can itself play a role in such evolution of feeling. As Rosenwein (2016) explores in her concept of 'generations of feelings', emotions, or at least their cultural representation and expression, can be lost and found over time. Old emotions can be re-encountered and given new life in the present, when they offer a way of thinking or feeling to a group that is productive. Emotions then can have long lives, moving in and out of 'fashion' and being co-opted and evolved for new environments as they come once more to the fore. Historical emotions that were 'lost' to mainstream cultures can also survive in smaller communities that hold on to particular traditions or practices over time.

If all emotions have histories, encounters with emotion in historical sources can produce a range of challenges for experts and non-experts alike. A key question for both revolves around how to recognise an unfamiliar emotion (Frevert, 2011). How do we interpret the emotions suggested on a face in a historical painting? How do we identify a word as an emotion word? Historians of emotion have produced a sophisticated set of methodologies to deal with these questions, many of which rely on developing a deep familiarity with the particular context in which such an emotion occurs. Art historians might turn to guides for artists that teach them how to display a particular emotion in their work; a historian might look to a dictionary or medical text; a literary scholar might read widely to understand how a particular term or behaviour was used and interpreted by authors. Often historians deploy all these practices and more as they set out to contextualise and interpret their records (Barclay, Stearns, & Crozier-De Rosa, 2020). Non-historians are less likely to have this training or the time and resources to perform this kind of analysis and so their relationship to representations of emotion can be quite different. For some historians, the responses of non-historians to past representations of emotion have been regarded as naïve. But a growing appreciation of the full range of contemporary encounters with the past highlights that such practices are fruitful sites for understanding how we engage with our histories (D'Arcens & Lynch 2018; Gerzic & Norrie 2018).

A growing scholarship now explores how people interact with history and represent the past in a range of environments, from museums to schools to books, film, and television (de Groot, 2016). As would be familiar to modern audiences, representations of the past are creative productions, drawing together strands of knowledge and surviving fragments of information into narrative, and deploying a range of rhetorical and generic rules to produce compelling art forms. This might include the use of fabulous costumes, humour and entertaining dialogue, and fictionalised events, people, or chronologies to enhance the story-telling power of a particular piece of work. All histories, in every genre, make selective choices about what should be included or left out. History's possibilities are also shaped by available sources, methodologies and researchers, and scholarly work can open up new insights on a topic or suggest a reconsideration of accepted truths. As such, historical works are always as reflective of our contemporary moment as the pasts that are told. They are moments where past, present, and sometimes future interact and shape each other.

Scholarship of transhistorical emotion has been especially interested in the emotions that arise from our encounters with the past, whether in curated productions (such as academic texts, films, or plays) or original source materials found in an archive or stored in an attic. Early forms of this scholarship – especially that which focused on non-academic histories – considered public interactions with the past through a lens of nostalgia, a yearning for what was lost that could be closely tied to sentimentalism and uncritical nationalisms (for discussion see D'Arcens, 2011; Dell, 2018). Empathy too has been important here, where engagements between actors across time are viewed as a form of recognition of 'the other' and a desire to understand their experiences, for better or worse (D'Arcens, 2018; de Groot, 2006; Moyn, 2006). Here the feelings we experience in relation to past peoples are not simply a product of our own imagination, but act to acknowledge the agency of the archival record and its impacts on the world. More recently, scholars have sought to consider emotions not as simple responses to stimuli but as part of knowledge-making and communicative practices. As such, the emotion 'work' performed in an encounter with the past can be viewed as producing new historical meanings and understandings.

As has been explored at length by D'Arcens (2014), humour has played a significant role in mediating our relationships with the past, allowing the public to laugh 'at, with, and in' a particular historical period, with different social and political effects. To laugh 'at' the Middle Ages, for example, might mark our superiority over the past and reinforce narratives of progress. More complexly, to laugh 'with' and 'in' the Middle Ages provides opportunities for people to negotiate the distance and nearness of past and present, to mark the incongruity of the unfamiliar, and the embrace of the seemingly universal. Such accounts might act as a critique on contemporary society, 'failing' in comparison to past peoples (e.g. Wilkins, 2014), or allow the exploration of our values and beliefs. Other emotions, such as the love developed for those studied, might enable a critical analysis of past behaviours, bringing out nuances of motivation and morality (Barclay, 2019b). New readings of nostalgia allow for the past to be recognised as part of the present and not simply held at a distance (Dell, 2018). Across these examples, emotions are understood as having pedagogical value that contributes to how the past is interpreted and becomes part of contemporary experience and knowledge.

As the past is deployed in the production of the present, whether as entertainment, social critique, or as common-sense knowledge of how the world works, so these transhistorical emotions become implicated in the construction of self, identity and community. Engaging with the past – whether through niche art forms targeted at small groups or as part of national histories – become part of how we interpret and make intelligible who and what we are today, and transhistorical emotional encounters facilitate that activity. In this sense, the histories we engage with, and especially those that facilitate an affective response, become technologies of the self, in the Foucauldian sense of devices that enable the social construction of identity. It can be suggested then that memes that deploy historical works to produce emotional responses in their audiences are similarly expressive technologies.

Extending the Self

Courbet used an etching by Dürer to enable his expression of melancholy; the Florida State University History Department in turn deployed Courbet's self-portrait to express contemporary feelings of unease with modern online environments. A 500-year-old gesture of desperation was not only transmitted across time but reconfigured to enable the emotional expression of individuals at very different historical moments. If representations of the past are opportunities for self-construction, then so too is the meme, a device deployed by communities of shared interest or identity, and which can be used to offer an account of the self and emotion to others. As previously discussed, the historical art meme brings together a historical source, typically a piece of art or illustration, and combines it with contemporary commentary, either lifted from recent popular culture, or produced by the meme creator and designed to be humorous, ironic, political, or otherwise thought-provoking (Aharoni, 2019; Raivio, 2016; Wilkins 2014). Used to build communities and to articulate personal emotions, experiences, and perspectives, the historical art meme can be located like other representations of the past as sites where people use 'the past' as a technology of the self. If this is the case, memes are perhaps distinct in providing a tool that is readily available for re-use in the everyday, can be collected and carried around on mobile devices, and deployed at appropriate moments to do identity work. A meme might be compared to clothing or a branded mobile technology whose efficacy lies not simply in acting as a resource to think with, but as an instrument that can be reiteratively and strategically deployed to display the self and its associations to others.

Here the insights of new materialists can be helpful. Scholars working within the framework of new materialism have attempted to overcome the popular binaries that are commonly used to understand human behaviour, including the distinctions imposed between the material world and language or discourse (Barad, 2003; Dolphijn & van der Tuin, 2012). They suggest that such a distinction is artificial and that language and the material world should be considered as mutually constitutive, and so can only be understood as an integrated whole, rather than in isolated parts. Such ideas have been important in the history of emotions as scholars have grappled with competing explanations of emotion as both a biological function and as a product of society and culture (Barclay, 2017). Rather than identifying emotion as the exclusive domain of either biology or culture, new materialist thinking moves past such dichotomies towards how the body and environment operate together, mutually informing and extending the other. Although influenced by a different philosophical tradition, Reddy (2001) has described this formation of emotion as a process of 'navigation', where physical sensations were interpreted through and adjusted to accord more closely to cultural norms for feeling. As Grosz (2011), drawing on Deleuze, puts it, 'life magnifies and extends matter and matter in turn intensifies and transforms life' (39).

As well as breaking down artificial barriers, new materialism emphasises the human-in-world, challenging the boundaries of the body and technology. Here the tools that humans use to produce themselves – whether the glasses that aid vision or the fashionable purchases that mark our inclusion in a particular social group – are recognised as extensions of the self, moving the boundary of the human beyond its fleshly limits (Braidotti, 2013; Haraway, 2013). Environment too has been theorised for its active role in shaping human behaviours, cultures, and outcomes. Just as rivers and mountains direct the travel of traffic, so too does environment impact on food cultures, health, language, and emotional repertoires. Local conditions, such as housing arrangements or family dynamics, direct behaviours and the social norms required to live successfully within them. New technologies then provide the opportunity to change and evolve behaviours, not least how we feel. For instance, the motor vehicle quickly came to be associated with 'road rage', a new emotion for new machinery (Matt & Fernandez, 2019). Digital media has similarly been recognised as a technology that acts to extend the human, where hardware devices, social media use, and digital animations and images work reciprocally with users to produce both selves and data (Lupton, 2019; Lupton, 2020). Emotion itself is increasingly theorised not simply as 'of the body', but a phenomenon that is enabled through the interactions of body, people, language, cultural beliefs, physical environment, technologies, and so forth (Barclay, 2020; Boddice, 2018). Emotions are enabled through practices that require tools, expressions, gestures, and props. The pretexts for emotion, how emotions are explained, and the conditions in which they are generated are viewed as integral to their interpretation and so their boundaries. Boundaries between the self and other dissolve.

A historical art meme, from this perspective, can be understood as part of the experience of emotion. As was explored above, memes are actively designed to produce emotional communities and as props that are deployed to communicate our feelings to others. This communicative effort is not simply a representation of emotion, but part of how emotions are constructed. Reddy (2001) describes expressions of emotion as *emotives*, speech acts that produce emotion through its naming and articulation. I speak of my anger and so feel anger. Similarly, when users express their emotion in meme form, the meme becomes an *emotive* that gives shape and form to abstract feelings. As memes become saturated with emotion and circulate, they produce, to use Sara Ahmed's (2004) framework, an affective economy. Memes instruct recipients on appropriate feelings and where such emotion should be directed, marking the boundaries of the emotional community. As Ahmed demonstrates for example, the emotions articulated by white supremacists were designed to produce the white community as a victim and rightful possessor of the nation, while simultaneously operating as an act of hate towards and exclusion of other racial groups. Likewise historical art memes can be understood as a communication of emotion that extends the self outwards to like-feeling others, while also – and depending on the subject at hand – acting as a boundary or limitation on an emotional community (Wilkins, 2014).

New materialist perspectives are also productive for considering the historical art meme as an engagement of past and present. The works of art and illustrations that are used as the foundational texts in these memes are chosen because – out of a myriad of others – something strikes a meme creator as potentially interesting, funny or, when combined with other texts, useful to make a point. Artworks can be chosen, like in other contexts (D'Arcens, 2014), because a text is 'foreign' yet 'familiar'. Many others offer images of behaviour that seem strange or bizarre to a modern audience, where the incongruity offers potential for humour. Modern behaviours, and especially emotional expressions, that seem out of context within a historical setting are also popular. These memes rest on an assumption that the past is a 'foreign country' and that the modern interpretation is necessarily anachronistic. That the past contains a 'foreign' aspect can also be rendered as surprising; histories are presented that cannot easily be placed into known historical narratives. The humour often arises in a supposed disjuncture between past and present. Not knowing the intention of the original artwork adds to the comic effect for many users; for others, pleasure can arise not only from 'getting the joke' but being able to contrast the modern interpretation with the artist's original intention, the pleasure of connoisseurship. Across examples, the past in the historical art meme is not simply collapsed into the present or passively redeployed for new ends but remains active in its alterity. This can be viewed as a form of material agency, where historical sources resist being lost to contemporary interpretation and remain distinct as products of past cultures.

Historical art memes provide examples of individuals and groups using the past as a mechanism through which to extend the emotional self. Memory practices, such as creating family genealogies or venerating war statutes, are noted to perform similar functions in identity-making, offering opportunities for histories to be reinterpreted for contemporary ends (Sutcliffe, Maerker, & Sleight, 2018). Less familiar is the explicit acknowledgement within the meme form that contemporary identity-making does not only emerge from a familiar and well-told story, but through a playful engagement with the past as unknown or surprising. Rather, the foreignness of the past can operate as a key opportunity to explore new selves, to comment on contemporary experiences, and to build or maintain emotional communities.

Playful Histories

Historical art memes cover a diversity of topics and themes: marginalia from medieval illuminated manuscripts; Renaissance sculpture; and paintings and drawings from the last thousand years, reflecting most of the key artistic movements across these periods. European high art is generally over-represented in English-language memes, likely because such art is more easily available to Anglophone meme-creators. Landscapes, particularly if they represent apocalyptic or similarly dramatic scenes, are sometimes used, typically in the context of commentary on current issues such as climate change or disaster scenarios. Satire and newsprints, which often contain a rich diversity of symbolism, irony, and humour, are less common, perhaps because they require a higher level of expertise to untangle. The large majority of memes favour portraits, and particularly group portraits, where those represented are allocated opinions, dialogue, and especially emotions and emotional responses. While some memes deploy pseudo-archaic words and phrases, the people represented are typically imagined as having modern sensibilities, politics, and perspectives. Thus, most memes rely on a conceit that the historical character is a 'modern' person out of place in time. This temporal connection between past and present offers an opportunity for the historical artwork to be deployed as a technology of the self for the modern user.

Due to the diversity of imagery, historical art memes can be used to comment on a wide range of contemporary experiences, events, and political issues, and so like other memes can be understood to serve a variety of functions. This Element points to two significant features that are suggestive of the emotional uses of the meme. Memes create emotional communities (Rosenwein, 2011); that is, they facilitate the building of a shared repertoire of emotional expression and valuation, and use representations of emotion to serve the social, political, or other communal functions of the group. Thus, frustrated, bored, or angry women are deployed as a social commentary on the present, and through being shared, 'liked', and commented on build agreement on a topic. Memes are also used to stand in for the emotions of the meme users. The category of memes that follow the pattern of 'when you [planned to do something commonplace] but [something intervenes]' involves a portrait of someone expressing what appears to be an appropriate emotion to the described scenario (see Figure 3). Here the individual portrayed in the meme, and their emotions, substitute for those of the meme creator; a historical person performs the emotions of the modern subject.

In both uses of the meme, a historical source and the emotions displayed within it are located at one step of remove from those whose feelings are meant

Figure 3 Figure 3 One example of this meme coupled Lucas Cranach's *Allegory of Melancholia* (1528) with the phrase 'When you planned to go out tonight but your friend has been pinged by the covid app and now she has to isolate'.

to be expressed. In some respects, this is not different from writing a love letter, where an embodied experience is given a physical form and a text comes to act as an intermediary between those communicating. Yet, the use of another's emotions is distinct here – the love letter (even when written by a clerk or guided by an advice book) at least purports to be the feelings of the author. These memes instead allow another to do this emotion work. Arlie Hochschild (2012b) in her discussion of the 'outsourced self' notes the phenomenon of using servants or services to perform emotional labour on a client's behalf, removing the inconveniences, vulnerabilities, and sometimes even undesirable feelings of managing personal emotions and those of others. If the subject of a historical portrait might similarly be viewed as an 'outsourced self', perform-ing similar functions to other emotions workers, the motivations, and effects of meme creators and users are somewhat different.

The historical art meme might rather be considered through a lens of 'mask-ing'. As Edson has argued, there are few societies in the world which do not use masks to explore their relationship to others, the divine and society (Roy, 2015). In using historical portraits, today's meme creators effectively challenge, recre-ate, and perform their own emotional identities without using their own faces. This type of mask usage has been well studied in the field of anthropology, where scholars such as Campbell (2000), Pollock (1995), and Tonkin (1979) have identified the use of historical and/or alternative faces as an important way in which individuals place distance between themselves and a message, and allow others to create their own meaning from the spectacle and performance. Tonkin (1979), for example, has noted that masks function to enable individuals to become an 'other' and to articulate power. Pollock (1995) argues that a key function of masks is to modify conventional signs of identity and focus attention on the ways in which identities can be displayed, revealed or hidden. Similarly, as Foreman (2000) notes, masks serve 'to liberate the wearer from the inhib-itions, laws and niceties of a seemingly well-ordered everyday life, but are also a reminder that chaos and destruction and mutability are always with us' (27–29). Many historical art memes use portraits as 'masks' to explore relationships between self and other, to build group identity, and to provide opportunities to explore and contest social order. Rather than avoiding the difficult emotions of the 'outsourced self', the 'mask' enabled by the historical portrait opens up opportunities to explore and articulate new feelings and new expressions of emotion.

The substitutionary effect of masking can be fruitfully considered through the lens of the ludic – play – where object-substitution has a central role with significant educational functions. Children use toys to practice the behaviours they observe and to explore different possibilities; adults use play to explore other dimensions of the self, new identities, or to renegotiate power (Piaget, 2014). Play offers an opportunity for feeling rules to be tested, explored, and extended. Carnival, where the ludic is deployed as a commentary and release from the expectations of the everyday, can become a site of political challenge and contest, safely contained within a recognised format (Li & Biommaert, 2020). Viewing historical art memes through a playful lens highlights the opportunities of this genre to explore new and old emotions and their expression. Given that many memes highlight distinctively modern experiences – mobile phone use, current events, friendship under contemporary conditions – and that the disjuncture between the now and the far past is critical to their humour, historical art memes can be understood to perform an educational function in allowing users to articulate and negotiate the appropriate – and inappropriate – responses to experiences for which precedent is not readily available.

If memes hold this function for the present, they also speak to our futures (for other examples of the past supporting this function see D'Arcens, 2014). As sites to test how people live, and to evaluate and respond to new experiences, memes contribute to a discussion about morality, politics, society, and the way things 'should be'. Emotional valence becomes central to moral assessments, where experiences that cause suffering are usually 'bad' and those that cause pleasure are 'good'. This itself indicates an emotional community built around a shared belief that emotion can be used as a measure of morality and so used to inform judgement and decision-making. Rather than relying on present feeling however, memes deploy the emotions of historical actors to frame and articulate current feeling, placing the weight of history behind the claims made by a meme user. Courbet's expressive face offers a possible option for the modern Zoom user and one that has the authority of 500 years of desperation.

4 The Emotions of Historical Art

Courbet's portrait resonates, at least in part, due to its aesthetic power. The large eyes and defined eyebrows, pink cheeks and lips on a pale face, the skilfully rendered hands tearing at his flowing hair, and the textured folds of his shirt, offer a striking image, made intimate by its scale – his face takes up most of the canvas drawing the viewer close. The emotion that he expresses, however, is more challenging to read. Where the title suggests desperation, a historicised reading of his gestures indicates a melancholic disposition. A modern reader might see alarm in the wide eyes, embarrassment in the pink cheeks and anxiety in the tearing of hair. The humour and effectiveness of the historical art meme relies on a reading of the bodies, gestures, and contexts of emotion that appear in an artwork. The text of the meme directs the viewer to the emotion on display and, in many instances, the efficacy of the meme relies on the audience affirming the reading offered by the meme creator. Much of the humour of the genre, however, lies in the instability of representations of emotion, especially across time, and the challenges of accurately reading bodies, faces, and gestures for feeling. The affirmation of the meme creator's reading of the image rests less on its historical accuracy than on its capacity to resonate with its audience. Sometimes this is because the meme creator identifies an emotional display that shares similar features to a contemporary emotion. At others, a particular situation lends itself to a humorous interpretation and the creator asks audiences to suspend their disbelief to embrace the joke. This section explores what is missed, or ignored, by meme creators in the pursuit of the joke – the original meaning of the text when it was produced – and explores why these images remain compelling despite this lack of context. If many viewers do not bring knowledge of the historical artwork's production and interpretation with them to their readings of the meme, nonetheless the past meanings attached to these images, not least the power of the 'face', retain a certain power in the present, which informs their cultural efficacy.

Emotions in Historical Art

The meaning of an artwork is informed by the cultural moment and artistic milieu in which it was produced, the original function of the work and the messages that it was expected to convey. Different traditions of painting and drawing adopted distinct representational strategies for the depiction of figures and things. Courbet's portrait, for example, suggests strong Romantic influences, despite his association with the Realist movement, and this association informs its interpretation today. Artist manuals, often including examples that have been redeployed today as memes, provided guidance on how to depict a particular emotional expression on the face or through gesture (Kendon, 2004). Courbet's expressive head is an example of an artist's exercise that used an older work, in this case by Dürer, as a model for emotional expression. While some artists sought to push boundaries or develop new styles, economic imperatives – being able to pay the bills – meant that many more artists produced work that conformed to conventional styles and art fashions that were desired by the market. This has left a rich resource of lesser-known artworks that are especially popular with meme users, because their content and histories are less widely shared and so the ambivalence around their meaning can be exploited.

Art was rarely designed to provide a simple duplicate of reality, but rather to tell a story that could be read by a culturally informed audience. Medieval works, for example, often contain religious allegories, offering a didactic guide to behaviour in visual form. The famous images of a 'nun picking phalluses from a tree', which appear as marginalia in a copy of the popular twelfth-century tale, *Romance of the Rose*, offer a female counterpoint to the male protagonist in the story (who pursues a 'rose', which is also a metaphor for female sexuality). If this superficially appears to be a tale of chivalric love, it is also replete with religious allegory – the penis-apple on the tree in the Garden of Eden marks sin and can be contrasted with the love of God (for discussion see Ehrhart, 1999). Realist paintings of the sixteenth and seventeenth centuries, especially from the Dutch Golden Age, similarly offered moral allegories, designed as commentaries on poor behaviour, love, or family relationships (Schama, 1987). Jan Steen's *The Drunken Couple* (c. 1655–65) showed an inebriated couple being robbed. In the vernacular of the day, a cat on the floor could be interpreted as a symbol of misconduct or danger, while the couple's foolishness was indicated by a picture of an owl, associated with poor eyesight and stupidity, on the wall.

Portraits of individuals often contained symbolism that gave clues to a person's identity. For men, this might include occupation, scholarly aspirations, or military prowess; for women, a portrait might offer information on family identity, occupation, or personal qualities like chastity, or leisured skills (Lovell, 1987; Retford, 2006). Many European paintings depicted scenes from the Bible, classical literature, and even contemporary novels or writings, relying on the public's familiarity with the episodes depicted. John Everett Millais's (1851–2) painting *Ophelia* references the character from Shakespeare's *Hamlet*. Eighteenth-century 'conversation' pieces offered group portraits set in naturalistic settings, but nonetheless were designed to speak to a group's social standing, interests, and embrace of fashionable values, like sensibility (Retford, 2017). Nineteenth-century realist paintings often provided social and political commentary on current issues; paintings of sailors injured at work or prostitutes on trains were designed to draw attention to contemporary 'problems' and to mobilise audiences to offer redress. Historical artworks are never simple representations of past peoples, but – like memes today – offer complex messaging that requires an informed reading.

Interpreting these images necessitates an appropriate education and often a close attention to detail. Clothing, for example, not only spoke to wealth and social status, but to morality, profession, and the relationship between individuals. An outfit considered risqué could signal that a woman was sexually available, but the interpretation was modified depending on whether she was portrayed with a group of women or alone with a man. Props in a room, from furniture, to food, to animals, might suggest the occupation or personal qualities of the subject portrayed, or contribute to a particular narrative of events being displayed. Symbols, such as family crests or religious iconography, could identify individuals and their associations with larger organisations or faith practices; some, like halos, or the position of hands, might signal that the person portrayed was a religious icon, or more commonly, deceased. Family resemblance could be important in portraits, especially for well-known or royal families. As portraits were used as propaganda and to promote love for the monarchy, being able to easily identify an individual as part of the royal family encouraged artists to emphasise shared or distinctive features (Barclay, 2021). Young children could be painted with their parents' faces (following that of their gender) to reinforce their lineal connection. The overarching meaning of any particular image emerged from this combination of contexts, clothing, props, and symbols, providing a narrative for the observer.

The physical body, especially the face, was not a neutral component within this scheme. The position of the body – whether it leaned or was upright, whether it displayed skin or was covered, how it related to others in the scene – all conveyed particular information to the spectator. Medieval and early modern works often used formal hand gestures to convey messages, following guidebooks that instructed artists in their significance (Kendon, 2004). The meanings of some of these gestures have now been lost, but many signified particular emotions, such as anger, wonder, and admiration. For example, the seventeenth-century portrait of Ferdinando II de Medici by Valore Casini and Domenico Casini shows a young man with his hand dropping towards the floor. This motion symbolised 'hope', an appropriate emotion for a young monarch with whom the ambitions of the nation lay. Gestures could signal a range of customary attitudes and behaviours, such as modesty, generosity, or fear.

Of all the parts of the body, the face often carried particular significance, not least in conveying emotion. Despite efforts by basic emotions theorists to identify a set of universal and transhistorical facial expressions, a history of the face demonstrates that displays of emotion have evolved over time (Downes & Trigg, 2017; Maddern, 2017; Rees, 2014). A classic example here is the history of the smile. For early modern Europeans, large toothy grins were associated with the lower classes, a lack of modesty, and at times even promiscuity. Contorting the face in laughter was taken to signal a lack of sophistication. By the eighteenth century, there was a developing trend for delicate smiles showing a small number of teeth, although careful moderation of expressiveness was still tied to respectability (Jones, 2014). A toothy grin that to contemporary eyes might appear to signal 'happiness' might have suggested promiscuity, disorder, or sinfulness to an early modern observer. Emotions in art could be highly stylised; just as a hand gesture might signal 'hope' or 'melancholy', so too a particular distortion of the mouth or facial muscles could come to stand in for an emotion. Here the multiple movements of the face when expressing a particular feeling were compressed into a single position that could be taught to artists and used across a variety of works. With changing expectations around the expression of emotion, some of these postures are no longer recognisable to us.

Skin colour and complexion mattered too. Not only was skin colour suggestive of race or ethnicity, but medieval and early modern medicine made an association between appearance and a person's humoral balance, which was believed to influence personality, morality, health, and behaviour (Koslofsky, 2014; Nyffenegger, 2018). Whether you were hot-blooded or cool, dry or wet, could be indicated in your hair and skin colour, as well as other bodily attributes, and could speak to temperament – hot blooded people were more likely to be red-faced and easily angered. The balance of the humours might be suggestive of deeply rooted personality traits but they could also be affected by more fleeting influences, such as a feeling of love, melancholy, or an over-active imagination. Whether a person was represented as flushed or wan could then offer messages to viewers as to personality or the immediate emotional dynamic in a scene. Even as medical ideas changed over the period, the association between complexion and behaviour continued as an artistic trope that viewers could interpret.

The representational complexity of historical art, and its use of stylisation to encourage specific readings of the image, can make these artworks seem inscrutable to modern audiences; however, it is this very inscrutability that makes these images so appealing to meme creators. The meme creator's interpretation of the image, particularly when tied to contemporary issues, leaves the historical readings readily visible to the viewer but unexplained – the past becomes the 'elephant in the room', the absent-presence that reinforces the incongruity of the meme-text. It is a critical assumption of these memes that the body and face can be read as a text by modern audiences.

Facework Today

The face has been given particular significance as a human symbol. For theorists like Levinas, the face was the first site of communication, preceding language, and so facial expressions held the potential for a universal connection (Downes & Trigg, 2017). The capacity for the face to communicate across time and culture has been significant to basic emotions theory that posits the existence of a small number of emotions that pre-exist culture and which everyone are thought to share. Following this idea, psychologists have conducted experiments that attempt to capture a generic expression of particular emotions that can be successfully read by all human groups (with limited success) (Boddice, 2018). The idea that facial expressions might be readily communicated across groups also underpins heavily stylised emotional faces, such as emoticons, which have become a widespread, cross-cultural language of emotion in the digital world (Bai et al., 2019). Yet, as this last example suggests, the success of the face as a site for feeling has rested less on an innate capacity to read such symbols, than in the cultural education that has accompanied their spread. In order to become fluent users, many groups have relied on the translation of emoticons, and it is well recognised that emoticons can be misused, often unintentionally and with humorous effects. Emoticons, like memes, rely on a shared cultural knowledge, and can be deployed to produce boundaries between 'insiders' and 'outsiders'. Thus, if many people, even today, have faith in the capacity of humans to read emotional expression in the faces of others, the practice of doing so has been more challenging. Rather, and as we suggest here, European culture's investment in the face as a symbol with communicative potential is both long-lasting and underpins its commitment to engaging with faces as transparent sites for emotion.

The capacity of the body and particularly the face to provide an access point to the 'inner' person is a long-established trope in European culture. Not only has art and literature across the centuries offered detailed accounts of physical form, gesture, and facial expression as a mechanism for telling something of the character represented, but such ideas were significant in everyday life, shaping personal interactions, decision-making, and the capacity to trust. Witnesses testifying in courtrooms, for instance, have traditionally been placed on boxes or stools to ensure that their bodies and faces can be 'read' as they speak and in this way the body is understood to affirm or deny the truthfulness of its words (Barclay, 2019a). That the observer can 'read' bodies and their emotions as suspicious or 'up to no good' remains a significant idea in policing, whether in identifying shoplifters or terrorists at airports (Plamper, 2015). The cultural anxiety in the West about face coverings often reflects these long-held beliefs in the body's capacity to 'speak' the subject, something that is perceived to be closed off through cloaking (see for example Marini et al., 2021). Not least, many contemporary psychologists persist in experiments that seek to identify expressions and gestures as representing particular emotions and chart the extent to which people can effectively identify such feeling through an observation of the body (Safra et al., 2020).

The body and face are understood as significant access points to the 'authentic' self, exposing more than we might wish to reveal and, more positively, offering the possibility of connection and communication between different bodies. These beliefs give representations of the human form a particular efficacy for viewers, where images of bodies and faces provide the potential for such connection. This is also true of representations of historical people, perhaps most poignantly expressed by family historians who articulate the power that family photographs have in reinforcing a sense of lineage and shared identity across generations (Sandbye, 2014). Notably, family photographs are often viewed as the more significant when they capture ancestors who are otherwise unknown. Looking upon an image of another is understood to provide an array of information that helps to fill the 'gap' of a lost relative.

As Louise D'Arcens (2018) suggests, the importance of physical representations of past actors to modern audiences has fed a demand for physical description and personal iconography. Television and film of the lives of historical notables often seek to provide a likeness to the person represented, sometimes a 'likeness' that speaks more to how a person is imagined than a biographically accurate account. Similarly, new technologies that can build suggestive representations of a person based on bone structure and that use DNA to make estimates of eye and skin colour are now received to popular acclaim. Where the skeletal remains used to reconstruct faces are lacking, nonetheless artists might attempt to recreate a historical person using surviving descriptions or drawings. Such faces are then used in museums and galleries to heighten the impact of displays of historical bodies or the artefacts of other cultures.

Deleuze and Guattari (1987) suggest that faces create a 'loci of resonance', 'the wall' for the viewer to 'bounce off' when constructing their reality, and so readings of the face are intersubjective and socially constructed, conforming to 'dominant realities' that change over time and place (p. 168; discussed in D'Arcens, 2011). Faces are also sites of communication and negotiation, where the viewer recognises 'the other' as someone distinct from themselves and so can consider the possibilities of a relationship with them. Both the face and body have the potential to enable an affective response from observers. This is not because they offer access to a universal humanity shared across time, or a recognition between two authentic selves, but because they enable a moment of recognition (where the face conforms to our cultural interpretation) and distance (in recognising the past actor as 'not us'). The affective response enabled by this process is not always positive, affirming a shared identity over time, but can – such as in the instance of an antagonistic cross-racial encounter – produce hate or racism. Rather, the affective resonance of the face arises due to its semiotic depth, its familiarity and strangeness, and the cultural weight bestowed upon it as a site where the self can be read.

Within the historical art meme, the face and body of historical people act as 'loci of resonance', encouraging affective connection and engagement with historical artworks. The historical artwork is interpreted by meme creators (and their audiences) through a modern paradigm of emotion. The alterity of the past, and the challenge posed by the other contextual material that forms the artwork, puts the dominance of this paradigm into question. The tension between individual and society, past and present, enhances the affective possibilities for meme creators, heightening the ambiguity of the reading that is at the heart of its humour. The past here is both surprising – in resisting contemporary paradigms – and yet still 'conservative', in that modern readings of past artworks provide the 'dominant reality' through which past bodies are read. This can have knock-on effects on the political functions of the meme, reinforcing narratives of progress where contemporary issues, around, for example, race, sexuality, or climate change cannot be envisioned as part of past society's experiences.

5 Emotions, Memes, and the Politics of Expression

The Courbet meme was not circulated by an individual but by the anonymous Facebook page administrator at Florida State University History Department, a role performed by a 'social media intern', likely a member of the university student body. As this suggests, memes are not simply used to express emotion by identifiable individuals, but rather circulate as part of an online economy that includes organisations, businesses, advertisers, interest groups, and private individuals. People communicate as themselves, as avatars, and on behalf of groups and corporations, and their interactions flatten distinctions between personal and corporate interests, just as the datafied digital world monetises our emotional lives online. Importantly, the digital world is a disembodied world, where expressions of emotion must be intentionally manifested by users – for others to know how we feel, we must write our feelings down, photograph ourselves with a suitable expression or gesture, use an emoji, or film ourselves as we display emotion in a recognisable form.

Mediated through the digital environment such expressions of emotion require careful curation; just as Courbet employed Dürer's desperate gestures because they held cultural resonance amongst an audience who could interpret their meaning, so contemporary digital media users are required to demonstrate feeling using agreed representations of feeling. Portraying emotion effectively in any art form is a skilled task and is more challenging for media profiles that represent groups or brands and where there is no representational individual easily available to provide digitised emotional expression. Digital cultures are therefore performative cultures, where human bodies, collectivities, and technological apparatuses fuse together and blur the boundaries between self and other, human and non-human, online and offline, private and public (Barad, 2003; Leeker, Schipper, & Beyes, 2016). We have argued in previous sections that the historical art meme offers a useful tool in these performances of self, offering a human form – in the shape of a historical person – as a mask for an online persona, whether it is used by an individual, a group, or a corporation. In this section, we extend this insight to explore the various functions of the historical art meme as it used to convey emotions on another's behalf. In the examples that follow, historical art memes use tronies and images of unusual faces as 'masks' that allow for a working through of the complexities of power, emotion and identity in the 'always on' digital age. Specifically, these faces are used to play out present-day performances of 'reacting', 'witnessing', and 'being seen' online.

Historical Art Memes 'React'

In 2017, HBO's multimillion-dollar medieval fantasy drama, *Game of Thrones*, aired an episode where a main character, Sansa, swiftly and unexpectedly enacted revenge on another, Lord Baelish, destroying an alliance and acting as a key moment in the former's character development. The show, a cult phenomenon, saw audiences across the world immediately respond, sharing their varied reactions on an array of social media. One such meme (Figure 4), made and shared on the day the episode aired, deployed Joos van Craesbeek's self-portrait, *A Man Surprised* (c. 1635), coupling the face of a man with wide eyes and an open mouth with the text: 'Sansa: How do you answer these charges … Lord Baelish?? Me: [blank]'. The surprised man of this portrait filled in the blank of the text, acting as a 'reaction meme' where people use another's facial expression in place of their own.

As a unique subset of online communication, reaction images and memes are explicitly used to build connections with others via humorous and sometimes ironic emotional responses to events that happen both on- and off-line (Schankweiler, 2020). Exaggerated, unusual, or grotesque faces are commonly used in reaction memes as a stand-in or proxy for the meme creator. Where some memes use the facial expressions of celebrities, actors, or domesticated animals (especially cats and dogs), historical art memes typically use the faces of historical actors from classical art. In this meme, van Craesbeek's face provides a comical, exaggerated, and ironic visual representation of 'surprise' that can be transferred onto a number of present-day experiences. Texts such as 'Me when I'm eating wasabi', 'When you're in the kitchen at 2 am and you drop a spoon',

Sansa: How do you answer these
charges...Lord Baelish??

Me:

Figure 4 Sansa How do you answer these charges? Reddit classical art memes
www.reddit.com/r/classicalartmemes, accessed 10 December 2021

and 'When your kid barges in your room without knocking and they see you and Mom "wrestling"' have also been applied to this image. Eyes wide, mouth open, Craesbeek's direct gaze, concentrated in a small box, invites the viewer to see his face as if it were their own mirror reflection, and it is precisely this possibility for identification that meme creators have readily taken up (Pollock, 1995).

The exaggerated expression is critical to the efficacy of the reaction meme as it clearly signals an emotional response. If subtle or vacant faces can act as a wall on to which emotion can be imagined (and historical art can be deployed in this way), highly expressive faces offer a useful mechanism for communicating an experience that might otherwise be fleeting or internalised, and so allow the exchange of feeling without significant textual or other apparatus. While the emotion depicted by the original artist might at times be ambiguous, meme creators assume a shared capacity to interpret particular gestures – an open mouth, wide eyes – as associated with specific emotional experiences, like surprise. That contemporary audiences often receive their emotional literacy through observing historical art has allowed such portraits to be deployed effectively as part of the reaction meme genre, and the circulation of such images in response to particular events reinforces how these faces should be read for emotion.

Joos van Craesbeek's *A Man Surprised* is a tronie that was originally a deliberate and emotive play on the concepts of surprise and self-reflection. The term 'tronie' stems from the early modern Dutch word for 'face' or 'mug' and refers to a popular and often irreverent artistic style that emerged within the Dutch Golden age and Flemish Baroque paintings of the era (Adams, 2009). Featuring exaggerated, unusual, and well-defined facial expressions, tronies were created to express abstract notions of identity and commonly played with concepts such as transience, youth, old age, race, gender, and social status. The arresting faces found in tronies provide a powerful expression of 'otherness' and ambiguity that cannot be easily captured in traditional portraiture or other contemporary forms of emotional self-performance, such as selfies or emojis, and provide a space where emerging emotions and transgressive experiences can be performed.

As a painter who was well known for his dissolute self-portraits, van Craesbeek took great interest in emotional self-performance and often painted himself with exaggerated expressions to convey a range of humorous, emotional, and sociopolitical affects. The reaction meme in Figure 4 is a similarly self-reflexive and self-deprecating commentary on surprise. The meme creator wishes to demonstrate their emotional investment in the television show, whilst also communicating their awareness of the triviality of such feeling. As a text, the meme demonstrates an intra-cultural knowledge of a set of emotions at play in a media event – in this case, episode seven, season seven of *Game of Thrones*. And it also provides a self-reflexive acknowledgement of how emotional expression is understood to be an inherently performative public act by today's digital audiences, and thus is required to communicate more than just feeling.

While the 'reaction' performed here is specifically related to a single scene in *Game of Thrones*, the scene itself is wholly absent from the meme. Rather, it is the experience of sharing and performing one's emotions and reactions to a media event that is of primary interest to the meme creator. As Schankweiler (2020) observes, it is common for reaction images to emphasise the activities of viewing and reacting while leaving the specific object of these activities outside of the visual frame. Understood in this way, the act of 'witnessing' a media event becomes an opportunity to attest and perform one's own state of being affected in the digital realm. It is precisely this situation that has led Schankweiler to note that the production of affect is usually the central point of reaction images (Schankweiler, 2020).

The emotions expressed in Craesbeek's self-portrait are meant to be interpreted by the *Game of Thrones* meme audience as a proxy for those felt by the meme creator during a moment of affective witnessing. Like the Gustave Courbet meme, previously discussed, the *Game of Thrones* meme works because it is what Schankweiler (2020) calls 'affectively contagious'. In other words, it encourages the millions of viewers who witnessed the Lady Sansa/ Lord Baelish scene to receive Craesbeek's emotions as their own. Viewed in this way, historical art memes extend the self. They do not simply seek to 'represent' their creators; they seek to *be* their creators, or, as Nash (2017) notes, we do not just 'engage' with the digital; we *are* the digital.

A striking aspect of this example is the speed with which the meme was created and shared and the ways in which that immediacy almost certainly resulted in a sense of 'real-time', collective experience for viewers of the show. In participating in an affective feedback loop of reacting and performing, the meme creator and their audience are drawn into a polysemic experience of representation that requires a high degree of cultural literacy and a robust understanding of the entwined emotional experiences of witnessing and react-ing online. The audience collectively felt surprise whilst watching *Game of Thrones* and the meme captured that shared emotion. Returning to Schankweiler (2020), we can see here a clear example of how image economies and affective economies are not just interconnected, but also interdependent in their quest for attention. The audience is implicated in a unique form of 'affective media witnessing' – a type of witnessing that becomes a collective and relational activity – a practice that creates communities through a shared sense of experience (Schankweiler, 2020). To use Ahmed's terminology, the sharing of this historical art meme engaged its audience in a series of affective dynamics that worked to 'align individuals with communities' in real time (Ahmed, 2014).

Ugly Mugs and Being Seen

Performances of reacting and 'being seen' online are also at work in Figure 5, which uses Jan Sanders van Hemessen's painting *The Weeping Bride* (c. 1540). The image chosen for this meme is an extreme close-up taken from a larger artwork that depicts an older woman weeping on her wedding day with a bridegroom and a young man standing on either side of her. Like many images used in historical art memes, the original painting is itself a satiric social commentary that uses demonstrative facial expressions and various motifs of debasement to communicate subversive and/or difficult emotions. It reflects on the theme of marriage at an advanced age and makes several coarse sexual references through the depiction of a chamber pot (commonly associated with sexual impropriety), a torn dress (likely a symbol of being claimed or seized by her husband/end of virginity), and a garland of cherries (ironically referencing female beauty and fertility when juxtaposed with an elderly woman with a visibly snotty nose). The message for the knowing viewer is of the fruitless-ness of marriage for an older couple, where a woman gives up her relative freedoms as a single woman to little advantage in coupling with an older man,

When you're getting roasted in the
groupchat but you type "lol" and
act like it's all good

Figure 5 'When you're getting roasted Hemessen meme', *Ahseeit*,
17 October 2018, https://ahseeit.com/?qa=48/when-youre-getting-roasted-in-
the-group-chat

while the concept of sexual congress at an advanced age is held out as disgusting
and so appropriate to ridicule.

There is a long history of using ambivalent, grotesque, and vulgar characters
as proxies for disempowered individuals, or as a form of critique on wider social
power relationships. As Stallybrass and White (1986) have argued, western
cultural texts and rituals that engage with power and transgression commonly
draw upon the symbolic extremities of the exalted and the base, depicting them
in humorous, incongruous, and playful forms and contexts. This can be seen in
both the original artwork and its meme form. Where the original artwork uses
the bride's image to parody the distinction between acceptable social norms (of
youthful marriage) and cultural/corporeal 'otherness' (represented by old age),
the meme furthers this sentiment by appropriating the bride as a proxy for the
meme creator who is in a state of dishonour. The script 'When you're getting
roasted in the group chat but you type "lol" and act like it's all good', coupled
with an unattractive, crying face, signals the disjuncture between the acceptable
response to ridicule of good humour and the bruised egos that many, in practice,
experience. The meme creator transforms vulnerable and 'uncomfortable'
emotions such as shame and humiliation into an entertaining and performative
act that generates empathy and social recognition. It engages in an advanced

relational practice that self-consciously references an individual experience of a shared social vulnerability, in this case, being teased online, while saving 'face' through the use of self-deprecating humour.

The reflexivity of this meme can be contrasted with those that are used to ridicule or criticise expressions of emotion online that are thought to be unbecoming or illegitimate. The Ducreux portrait (Figure 2), for example, has been coupled with the phrase 'art thou enraged, kinsman?' a pseudo-archaic translation of the popular 'u mad, bro' meme, as a 'reaction' to respond to people who appear to be overly defensive, or become irritated, as part of an online conversation. It is not dissimilar to the 'cry more' meme, which taunts people who are seen to be complaining online. In both instances, these reactions are disciplinary in alerting social media users that their emotional expression is unbecoming, illegitimate, or poorly received. What is at stake here, however, is not the expression of emotion itself, but that users have momentarily forgotten the rules of the digital domain and forgotten to maintain one's image.

Given this, the use of 'ugly' faces such as in *The Weeping Bride* meme is significant. Meme humour often has a vulgar and liminal quality that is reflective of many ritualistic performances throughout history (Campbell, 2000). With its emphasis on the grotesque, the bride's face reveals an identity in flux. The openings of the body, in this case, the mouth and nostrils, are emphasised, as are the body's secretions (tears and snot). Through the ridiculed bride, the audience can engage with the meme creator's experience of being humiliated online with a sense of both repugnance and fascination – the bride becomes a representation of a degraded and vilified self. At the same time, by presenting oneself for ridicule, the bride/meme creator maintains the upper hand, if briefly, in this negotiation of power.

Affective witnessing is again at play here, but this time the importance of emotion is heightened even further. While the *Game of Thrones* meme relied on a shared witnessing of a popular show – even if that happened offline – *The Weeping Bride* meme does not require any personal knowledge of the underlying events that caused an individual to be 'roasted'. Rather, the meme creator places an emotional experience at the forefront of communication; the meme's sole purpose is to highlight a generic emotional experience and to use a shared recognition of that emotional experience as a mechanism for producing connection and community. Since the shared experience here is perceived as typically disempowering, the meme is able to operate as a site of resistance and contest to online norms of self-presentation, and the use of self-deprecating humour offers the meme audience a mechanism for expressing such feeling without losing the recognition of their community.

WHEN YOU FART DURING YOUR ZOOM LECTURE
AND FORGET TO TURN OFF THE MICROPHONE

oh shit

Figure 6 'When you fart on zoom meme', *MeMe*, https://me.me/i/oh-shit-
9640c43c2efb4fd880febd88a18c0b9d

Other memes perform similar work through the deployment of 'low' or 'toilet' humour. Figure 6 combines a gallery view of the video-conferencing platform, Zoom, with nine expressive historical portraits seemingly responding to someone farting without putting their microphone on mute. Taken from a painting by Fra Bartolomeo (c. 1510), the meme 'creator', guilty farter, appears centre screen as Saint Thomas Aquinas. Around him is a collection of famous portraits, especially chosen for their expressive faces. These include Rembrandt's *Portrait of a Scholar* (1631), Jenő Gyárfás' *Study of Abigail's Head* (c. 1880), and William Powell Frith's *Lady Mary Wortley Montagu* (1852). Perhaps suggestive of an academic environment, the figures conversing by Zoom represent cultural elites known for their contributions to religious piety, art, literature, and intellectual culture or governance, and so the suggestion of the 'fart' acts to debase the scene and refigures their expressions as a response to this event. Humour of the 'lower body' has been central to the performance of unpleasant, liminal and transgressive emotions for centuries (Stallybrass & White, 1986), and through its expression of a universal experience is deployed to disrupt or contest social order. Here 'the fart' expresses the anxieties of a public getting to grips with a new medium of communication, showing the risk it presents for personal humiliation and skewering the imagined pomposity of a particular intellectual milieu.

Emotions such as bodily shame, social humiliation, annoyance, humour, and disdain manifest as moments of ambivalent play in the digital sphere, where the vulnerability of these 'ugly' emotions offers a moment of opening and human connection. To paraphrase Frosh and Pinchevski (2014), shared vulnerability is now a cultural currency in the digital realm and offers an opportunity, if briefly, to refigure or contest its rules. Yet, like the emotionally charged spectacles of carnivals, sideshows, fairs, and freakshows, while these memes allow users to articulate anxieties, fears, and resentments that rail against the norms of digital culture, they ultimately reinforce ubiquitous power structures. Memes, like the traditional carnivalesque performances that temporarily disrupted religious and social conventions, can ultimately be understood as licensed, permissible forms of hegemonic rupture or a contained 'letting off steam'. As Eagleton, quoting Shakespeare, has noted (1981, cited in Stallybrass & White (1986)), 'there is no slander in an allowed fool'.

This becomes particularly pertinent in the ways these moments of vulnerability ultimately reinforce the centrality of the self and its (emotional) presentation to a digital culture marked by 'selfie culture' and 'instagrammable' lifestyles. The grotesque found in memes like that of *The Weeping Bride* share features with the online aesthetics of 'internet ugly', which, according to Douglas (2014), normalises a flawed and unpolished visual appearance as a way of mocking mainstream conventions. Using tropes such as poor grammar and misspelling alongside rough image editing, and oddly sized font, the internet ugly aesthetic is identified by Douglas as a deliberate imposition of 'messy humanity' upon the tidy online world of smooth gradients and imperfection-correcting digital tools such as Photoshop and Autocorrect. The use of grotesque features or low humour redeploys the historical carnivalesque as a form of 'internet ugly' for the contemporary world, and the subversive intent of the 'internet ugly' is given the power of the carnival in offering a moment of rupture. The historical art meme operates through a series of oppositions – familiar but unfamiliar, vulnerable but self-deprecating, past and present – that push and pull on their audience, keeping them close and holding them at a distance. This is the power of the historical art meme as a 'mask', where the power of masking is not disguise but opportunity, albeit momentarily, for a refiguring of relationships, identities, and power.

Always On

While the always on, always performing aspect of digital life brings new opportunities for emotional engagement, it also adds a layer of complexity to conventional understandings of how we emote online. In an era where every online interaction is tracked, measured, saved, and monetised, today's internet users express their emotions within a system that requires them to perpetually reflect on and monitor their own emotional performance (Cover, 2015). There are considerable concerns around the perpetuity of online existence and 'digital footprints' and many schools and workplaces now offer training around 'appropriate' and 'safe' digital interactions. Online expressions of rage, jealousy, or hatred, for example, can have a significant afterlife and may resurface years or decades after their expression, often with negative or unforeseen consequences for those involved. Employers are known to monitor social media profiles, as are potential lovers, journalists, and law enforcement agencies. In the digital realm, emotions do not simply stay neatly contextualised at a particular moment of origin; they refract and reverberate through time, taking on different meanings as they are applied to new and evolving contexts.

Just as individuals perform emotions in ways that require self-reflexivity across time and space, so too does art itself. As art has become imbricated with digital technologies, artists and curators have been encouraged to critically reflect on the temporality of art and its evolving techno-social capacities. As McQuire and Radywyl (2010) have argued, the digital realm has bought about a major shift in both art production and exhibition practices which involves a move away from the paradigm of 'representation' in which the artwork 'is by definition a belated response to an event' and towards a 'relational aesthetics' that foregrounds unfolding social relationships and events. They argue that art in the digital realm has become an 'ambiguous amalgam of the living and the dead'. Nash (2017) similarly suggests that contemporary encounters with art now exist in a state of 'unpolarised, latent ambivalence' – a zone of creative indifference – which requires mediation, or an 'encounter with an individual to bring it to life'. Drawing on Agamben (2013), Nash points towards the perpetual 'afterlife' of images where what 'has been' fuses together with the 'now' to create a new constellation of matter and meaning.

Bringing historical artworks and emotions into conversation with contemporary digital media facilitates a unique kind of emotional communication, one that not only understands the emotional nuances of 'always connected' contemporary audiences but also emphasises the participatory and performative nature of identity in the digital age. While using images as a testament to having witnessed or experienced an emotional event is not a new concept, the broad audience reach and real-time capacities of digital media platforms such as Reddit, Facebook, YouTube, and Twitter have dramatically intensified the process (Schankweiler, Straub, & Wendl, 2018). This intensification facilitates a unique temporal connection between the present and the past in the historical art meme, offering meme creators the opportunity to deploy faces and images of the past as a proxy of the modern self.

In recognising the 'always on' dynamics of today's digital culture, Frosh and Pinchevski (Frosh & Pinchevski, 2014) have observed that 'witnessing' in contemporary media involves a new configuration of mediation, representation and experience that transforms our sense of time and historical significance. In the examples used here, the self-reflective, intertextual, and often satirical modes of emotional expression that result from having our identities constantly online emerge. That digital media users employ agents from other times and places to stand in for their own emotions speaks to the immediacy of our current need to emote and be seen performing that emotion. It evidences a culture in which affective dynamics and relationalities are inherently tied to an individual's experience of having a particular emotion and being able to show or normalise their experiences through references to cultural norms and signs. Using a historical actor to stand in for emotions that are new, raw, or vulnerable provides a strategic distance and degree of safety for the person expressing that emotion. It also provides the space to make a joke or political comment that is at once removed from one's own face yet purports to be a direct expression of one's personal feelings.

The decision taken by meme creators not to use their own faces tells us much about the perceived vulnerability of displays of emotional expression in the digital realm and our desire to belong to coded and carefully guarded communities of shared interest. That we do not show our own faces after we fart and/or feel embarrassed in a group chat or watch a shocking television episode highlights the ongoing expectation that physical appearances on digital media should conform to 'idealised' models of beauty and consumption. Here the 'internet ugly' expressed by the historical portraits enables the performance of emotional vulnerability, without destabilising online personas that are, at least in part, rooted in stylised photographs of the model self. In doing so, they enable the emotional displays that support online communities and provide space to express and explore uncomfortable feelings or responses to changing social environments. Indeed, just as we might view historical representations of faces and emotions as culturally and politically coded, the digital era's reading of faces and emotions is shaped by its own particular codes and conventions.

6 Gender Politics and the Emotions of the Face

If memes can be deployed by individuals as extensions of the self, they can also be used by groups to enable emotional communities, reinforcing their collective commitments and activities. The capacity of the meme to act as a form of political critique and to share such attitudes and opinions rapidly across a group of like-minded people has been noted, not least in the study of political communities. As we explore in this section, feminist groups have routinely deployed a wide range of memes to create community, to stage political commentary, and to promote reform of patriarchal forms of social organisation (Breheny, 2017; Rentschler & Thrift, 2015). The success of this activity has been subject to some debate: on the one hand, feminist memes are often widely circulated and enjoyed across the political spectrum – the humour can be appreciated even when people do not agree with the underlying sentiment. On the other hand, the limitations of memes, their difficulty in conveying complex or ambiguous ideas, and that their take-up does not always signal agreement have been considered to limit their political efficacy. The meme, as noted in relation to the carnivalesque, can be read as inexorably conservative, acting as an outlet for emotion, but leaving the status quo largely unchanged (Hill & Allen, 2021).

This section focuses on the use of historical art memes as social commentaries on anti-social male behaviour. We look at three memes in high circulation, where an engagement between men and women in the painting is reinterpreted for a modern audience, enabling humorous political commentary. As in the examples previously described, the dynamic between past and present is deployed as central to both the humour and the social commentary presented by the work. Past emotions, especially as read from women's bodies, become central to the message of the text, reinterpreted for contemporary ends and to enable a sense of group belonging. Importantly, if the feminist critiques promoted by individual memes are not on their own able to offer social transformation, their rapid circulation and reuse come to shift assumptions around what gendered behaviours are acceptable, and so the evolution of the meme brings with it the possibility of a transformation in social attitudes.

Shared Experiences over Time

Many feminist memes, and indeed other popular cultural forms, locate gender inequity and sexual harassment and associated behaviours, as persistent problems with a long history. That the form, shape, and impact of gender inequity have varied over time and place is secondary within this account to a narrative of imperfect progress, where women's lives have improved but gender equality has still not been reached. While many feminist analyses of women's experience emphasise the role of patriarchal structures in producing systemic disadvantage for women, it is notable that in the historical art meme, patriarchy comes to be embodied by badly behaved men. Historical art memes are conspicuous in rarely providing commentary on the most serious impacts of gender inequity, such as rape and sexual violence, addressing instead what might be described as everyday 'micro-aggressions', like the refusal of men to permit female autonomy, knowledge, or right to personal space, or drawing on significant, yet commonplace, tropes such as the gender pay gap or an unequal division of labour in the household. Often bringing a feminist commentary to scenes of everyday life between men and women, historical art memes can be read as conservative in drawing attention to 'bad characters', more than systems or structures, and this likely accounts for their general popularity. Yet, the very familiarity and ordinariness of the topics – the often subtle, but sexist, treatment of women by men – arguably constitutes a radical gesture insofar as the meme calls attention to experiences that were, until recently, seen as too trivial for sustained political attention.

Some of the most popular memes on this topic are based on Berthold Woltze's 1874 painting, *The Irritating Gentleman* (Figure 7). This work depicts a scene on a train where an adolescent woman dressed in mourning clothes and with tears in her eyes is addressed by a large-whiskered man, smoking a cigar. The jocular

Figure 7 Berthold Woltze (1829–1896), *Der lästige Kavalier* (The Irritating Gentleman) (1874), oil on canvas, 75 × 57 cm, Private collection. Wikimedia Commons

looking man, several decades older, is standing behind her, leaning over her seat and shoulder, his cigar at her eyeline. That his attention is unwanted is marked not only through her body language – her back is to him and she is resolutely looking away from him and towards the viewer – but the series of contrasts the image presents. She is young, petite, dressed in black, seated and upset; he is large, standing, happy, considerably older, with abundant whiskers and a large red bowtie. The inappropriateness of his behaviour is reinforced by his incapacity to regulate his own emotional expression in response to her demeanour – he does not appear to be offering sympathy but humour.

The Irritating Gentleman was one of a number of 'problem pieces' produced in the late nineteenth century, designed to encourage a dialogue amongst the public about 'what was going on', how the scene should be interpreted, and the appropriate response of the characters within it. Its theme reflected broader concerns of the era about the ways that public transport, like trains, created opportunities for men and women, and people of different social classes, to meet in a context where the rules for encounter were still under negotiation and so fraught (Letherby & Reynolds, 2005). Was it appropriate to introduce oneself to a strange woman on a train, or was this beyond the boundaries of polite behaviour? If so, would one lean over a chair, or join her in her own compartment? Should one smoke on a train, especially if women were present, or should smoking carriages be introduced for this practice? Regardless of general rules, this painting makes clear the need for nuance in social interactions, particularly when a fellow traveller might be vulnerable or in distress. The irritating gentleman's behaviour was meant to be condemned.

The debates around good behaviour on public transport that shaped the production of the original painting have largely been lost to modern audiences, who hone in instead on the overbearing gentleman and the woman's distress. Instead, the painting resonates with images used as part of current debates around men's use of public space, particularly 'manspreading', where men sit with their legs apart and so take up more physical room than a woman in an equivalent situation (Jane, 2017; Lutzky & Lawson, 2019). The critique of manspreading emerged within the digital realm, supported by the sharing of images and later memes that include real examples of men in such a position, especially on the tube or a train. We can see similarities in the use of Woltze's painting to spark light-hearted, yet serious, political debate and these more recent images, designed for a modern digital world. What offers continuity between past and present is men's unwillingness to pay attention to how their bearing and gestures shape the experience of women around them, especially in public places.

Several memes allocate dialogue to the irritating gentleman, who ventriloquizes dull topics that are nonetheless thought to be popular among men today: 'Bcash is the real bitcoin'; 'let me tell you about my fantasy team'. Such phrases are designed to connect the historical content to a contemporary phenomenon, a juxtaposition expected to be humorous. Yet, the resonance of this scene is such that many people feel such additions are unnecessary to the key message it gives. Instead, it is shared by people across the gender spectrum with phrases that reinforce this encounter as a known universal: 'a painting that captures perfectly the essence of what it is like to dare exist as a woman'; 'we all know him'; 'Some things never change'; 'Every single woman has worn this face. EVERY. SINGLE. WOMAN.'; 'Woman have been harassed FOREVER that shit has the [*sic*] stop' (see the thousands of responses to this image being shared on Twitter at WikiVictorian, 2021). As much as humour, a surprising familiarity is central to the meme's efficacy, where what is required of the viewer is not to put aside their disbelief and read a historical text as modern, but the spontaneous recognition of a remarkably modern scenario. As one commentator noted, 'It feels contemporary in a lot of ways.'

As this commentary suggests, the distress of a young woman in mourning, irritated by inappropriate behaviour on a train, is universalised by these memes into a long-standing female experience of having to manage unwanted male contact, and one that should no longer be acceptable in the modern world. The body language and emotional expression of both parties are situated as easily interpretable for modern audiences. The past is not strange or 'other', but offers a continuity of gendered oppression, and it is this very continuity that under-scores how urgently change is needed. Historical emotions, particularly suffer-ing, become resonant as they are placed into a longer narrative of progress stalled, and where an emotional community is produced through a shared agreement that this is a politicised site of wrongdoing and necessary redress. The visual nature of the source material is significant here; it is less what the man says than his lack of social awareness and overbearing behaviour that is the problem, just as with manspreading imagery. The capacity of this image to express the woman's vulnerability and distress, when confronted with the man's jocular presence, generates a powerful sense of discomfort that can be hard to put into words but is legible to a modern audience primed by cultural critiques of men's use of space.

Shared by individuals who tie it to their own experience – 'we all know him' – this meme becomes an outlet for feminist feeling. The emotions of a young nineteenth-century woman are represented as those of women today, offering a safe distance between their own distress and its online expression. In an online environment where women are subject to considerable levels of violent threats, trolling, and other sexist and exclusionary practices, the use of a young, respectable, and vulnerable female subject supports the safety of meme users through offering them a layer of anonymity (it is not their face or emotion) and a compelling 'victim', the latter not least reinforced by the historical context of the painting. Modern assumptions about nineteenth-century woman as domestic creatures, in need or protection and with limited social and political agency, reinforce a reading of the inequitable dynamics of gendered power in this image – of overbearing men and women as victims. Accompanied by capitalised phrases (that signal strong emotions, especially anger) or with a demand for justice, the suffering explored in the 'irritating gentleman' memes supports a righteous anger and demand for change. Historical emotion is given new life for modern meme users as it circulates for personal and political ends.

Misreading the Face

Woltze's *Irritating Gentleman* would not have been interpreted in identical terms in the nineteenth century, or at least not by everyone. A young woman travelling alone and in distress on a train would be viewed as in need of protection from louts like the man who so impolitely accosted her but was less likely to have been read as a feminist critique of the micro-aggressions that infringe on women's freedom of action. The level of distress displayed by the woman in this painting can be seen, at least in part, as a result of being in mourning and thus it is the failure of the male protagonist to recognise this that constitutes a lack of propriety. This is somewhat different from the memes to which this painting is sometimes compared. One of these memes shows a clearly bored woman standing in a nightclub being talked at by a man, who like the male figure in Woltze's painting lacks self-awareness. A nightclub is at least an appropriate moment and location for such action, even if the man's attentions are unwanted. If these differences suggest that past and present do not overlap as tidily as the meme hopes, nonetheless the continuity of similar male actions ensures that the modern uses to which Woltze's painting are put do not feel too anachronistic. Other historical art memes, however, less readily identify the emotions of the historical context, layering modern emotions onto past actions and, in so doing, misrecognising past feelings. Historical emotions are given a continuity in their expressions and gestures, but their meaning is rewritten.

The painting *Contemplation* (1905) by the French artist, Félix Armand Heullant, offers a useful example. In it, a couple sit closely together on different chairs, but with their backs to each other. He reads his newspaper; she looks upwards from her novel with an expression that is often read as annoyance, frustration, or anger (Figure 8). *Contemplation* has been especially popular as a feminist meme, typically used as a commentary on the challenges women face in finding time for uninterrupted reading. One version of the meme combines

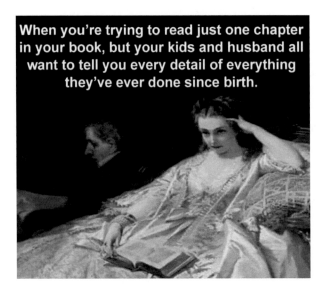

Figure 8 'When you're trying to read Heullant meme', Reddit, 7 August 2020, www.reddit.com/r/trippinthroughtime/comments/i5d4lf/are_you_done_yet/

the painting with the text 'When you're trying to read just one chapter in your book, but your kids and husband all want to tell you every detail of everything they've ever done since birth'; another condenses this sentiment into a dialogue: 'Did you see in the paper', he asks; 'So help me if he interrupts me one more time . . .', she thinks. A longer text that accompanies the painting on a Facebook version of the meme finishes this thought, 'she's just trying so hard not to murder him but honestly if she did and her case was heard by a jury of actual peers, which is to say fellow readers, they might decide it was justifiable homicide'. For contemporary readers, the emotions expressed in this scene are one of frustration, even anger, at being interrupted while reading. It is an interpretation of events that resonates: 'I feel this very strongly'; 'I have felt some variation of this emotion my whole life'; 'That's exactly what that look says', people of all genders commented in response to its circulation (see for example the comments on the Facebook post of this meme on Classic Art Memes Group 17 September 2021).

The frustration of being interrupted while reading is not distinctly gendered as the varied responses to these posts suggest, but much of the political edge of this meme reflects a common awareness that women have less leisure time than men, and that their reading is more likely to be subject to such interruptions, from children and other family members who need attention. Circulated on Facebook pages dedicated to various sorts of fiction (e.g. vampire fiction, romance), it perhaps especially resonated with those who identified as readers and who form part of a readerly community. But it was equally apparent that the meme's efficacy reflected its feminist undertones: 'He was mansplaining something', observed one commentator. Here this meme can be easily situated alongside many others, including *The Irritating Gentleman* above, which comment on men's unseemly behaviours.

A historicist reading of this work would lead to a rather different interpretation. This painting followed in a long tradition of those that commented on the problems with a May–December marriage, where young women were married to older men. An important subject of eighteenth- and nineteenth-century art and literature, the May–December marriage was typically viewed as signifying convenience – usually financial – rather than romantic love. The rise of such works reflected a growing emphasis on the value of love within marriage and the desirability of a companionate relationship that would support a family and household (Goodman, 2005). *Contemplation* shares several common motifs with other works on this theme that would have helped viewers of the period interpret the events before them. The younger woman and older man are in close proximity, indicating marriage; the spilled jewellery signalled wealth but also disorder; and the independent reading, reinforced by the couple with their backs to each other, can be compared with the more harmonious option of reading aloud from the same text. All of this imagery was common to an iconography of the May–December marriage.

The emotions being expressed by the female subject are therefore somewhat different to those allocated to her by modern viewers. Far from being annoyed by his interruptions, the young bride is frustrated by his lack of attention, and particularly a lack of sexual attention. This would be evident to a reader of the period by her dress, which – despite its frippery – was designed for informal and intimate occasions with close friends and lovers, rather than for formal or public occasions (see Gerbi, 2022 for this reading). Unlike many outfits of the period that would have been pinned (and so more challenging to undress), this is tied by ribbons, which suggests that this outfit can be easily removed. The female subject's positioning on a couch, supported by a cushion, resembled those where lovers met, and was designed to remind the viewer of the possibility of sex in such a location. In this sense, this painting acts as a commentary on the sexual incompatibility of those in the May–December marriage, where older men were thought to be less interested in sex and their young brides tempted to seek sexual satisfaction elsewhere. The audience of the period might have read this as a warning against such relationships, but even if they did not share such a prurient concern, they would have known that finding the time to read was not the female subject's main concern.

It could be argued that both historical and contemporary readings of this image identify frustration as the main subject's primary emotion, even if the conditions of its arousal were different, and so this example could be read as another case of emotion being successfully communicated across generations. However, the modern predisposition to read this image as concerning the frustrations of interruption, and not sexual satisfaction, is worthy of comment. There are several reasons for their misinterpretation. Firstly, reading this painting through a nineteenth-century lens requires some specialist art historical knowledge that a modern viewer cannot be assumed to possess. Secondly, and perhaps more importantly, this misrecognition reflects the meme's role as part of wider discussions in the feminist historical art meme community. In this setting, artworks are read in a purposive (rather than historicising) manner, to provide an interpretation that supports change to gendered behaviours today. Thus, the historical accuracy of the interpretation is diminished in order to accentuate the political agenda of contemporary feminists. Finally, it also reflects that a narrative of continuity of female oppression over time, and of progress in gender equality as a marker of modernity, lends itself to conservative readings of past behaviours.

A story of female sexual frustration, especially one that was not hidden within a private diary to be uncovered by a historian, but displayed in public works of art, held in major galleries around the world, offers a history of the nineteenth century that is less well known by modern publics. Moreover, it is a history that disrupts a story of progress that the feminist historical art meme wishes to deploy for political purposes. The past is a time of gender-based repression; sexist behaviours today are old-fashioned and not appropriate for the modern world. That nineteenth-century social commentators might have worried about women's sexual frustration and the importance of marriages that offered emotional and sexual fulfilment might suggest that gender relationships in the past were less repressive than we imagine. At the very least, a historically informed reading of Heullant's painting, challenges any straightforward history of continuity and progress.

Acknowledging this history would not only have disrupted the logic of the feminist historical art meme but may have made its public efficacy more challenging. On the one hand, the history lover might enjoy a more of-the-period reading of the image, but whether they could have then used it as a commentary on their own frustrations and feelings is more uncertain. A discussion of female sexual frustration is a meatier topic than everyday sexism, and, in an era of easy divorce, harder to blame on men's actions alone. The primacy of consent for sex in contemporary feminism eschews any requirement that a partner, male or female, might be required to provide sex and to publicly complain of such feelings could be viewed as rather hurtful of a partner, especially when in the form of an easily circulated meme. Sexual frustration is not easily turned into a meme by contemporary audiences; the problems with men interrupting your reading is safer territory.

The capacity of historical emotions to translate into the present is shaped not only by familiarity with the contexts of their production, but by their availability to be transmuted in ways that respond effectively to contemporary needs and conditions. Reinterpreted for present purposes, historical emotions provide the space to explore appropriate feelings to contemporary political conditions, and to give them the weight of past experience – my current frustrations are also those of my ancestors and so hold a legitimacy that reinforces critique. Deployed in the mode of a meme, such explorations are both playful and liminal, allowing people to extend their present frustrations into fantasy. A woman looking up from her novel becomes not only evidence of frustration, but anger and elaborate daydreams of murder – a killing that a 'jury of actual peers' would find justifiable. Such a scenario is both unlikely and extreme but offers substance to a claim of frustration over something that is so easily viewed as trivial, even harmless. Circulating and responding to such memes offers spaces to explore feelings that are commonly recognised but not always valued as politically important, and to suggest that things might change.

Future Forward

'Might change' is not a pattern for the future and one of the critiques of memes has been that even if they shine a light on contemporary problems, they are not able to offer any solutions. Yet, as D'Arcens (2014) notes of other uses of the past in the present, the past itself provides alternative ways of living and imagining, and certainly holds forth the possibility of change. The universalism of emotion in feminist memes does not typically offer the variety of feeling that a historian of emotion might wish for. However, such memes do contribute to shifting attitudes and ideas around gendered behaviours and to the production of emotional communities that operate on a shared set of values. It is challenging to measure the impact of such change, especially in the short term, but the repurposing of some feminist memes for alternative political functions is suggestive of their spread and impact, as is the online support for those that achieve viral status.

An example of a feminist historical art meme achieving widespread impact is the 'women so mysterious' meme, which employs a painting of William Blathwayt IV and his wife Frances Scott walking in the grounds of their

Figure 9 'Women so Mysterious Blathwayt/Scott meme', Facebook, The Female Lead, 27 November 2020, www.facebook.com/thefemalelead/photos/ so-mysterious-/2709873155942572/

home, Dyrham Park (Figure 9).[4] The text of this meme, or a version of it, circulates quite widely, attached to other images or without any picture at all. The originating source is unclear, but the Blathwayt/Scott adaptation discussed here appears to be one of the more popular versions. In the portrait, the 'mysterious women' motif is refracted through the couple's dialogue: 'Women are so hard to read', he says; 'Well actually we just wan … ', she replies; 'Such complex creatures'; 'If you just list … ', 'So mysterious'. The subtext is that women have in fact been quite explicit about their desires and demands for equality and fair treatment, but men are not listening.

The choice of the Blathwayt portrait is worth noting. The image itself is not especially remarkable, one of several hundred similar images of married couples produced over the eighteenth and nineteenth centuries. Nor is the body language or expression of the female subject especially suggestive that she is annoyed or frustrated. The original intention of the artist was likely to show her as a devoted wife; her face and body turns towards him, as he looks out

---

[4] This identification is that of the National Trust who owns the image: www.nationaltrustcollec-tions.org.uk/object/453816.

over his estates. The couple here signify the fulfilment of their expected gender roles within marriage and the achievement of a harmonious household. Comments on the meme as it circulates do not especially comment on the couple's deportment, although some extend the 'fantasy' scenario, usually by commenting on men's related behaviours (see for example responses to this meme when shared on Facebook by The Female Lead, 27 November 2020). It appears then that what is important for the efficacy of this meme is less historical emotion as displayed on the body, than that this couple's performance of the companionate marriage can come to stand for a conservative, non-feminist past that still resonates in the present. That he looks forward, rather than at her, while she waits patiently on him, reinforces the idea that men are not paying attention to the women at their sides. The choice of this image, over so many others, may also reflect on his fashionably large hat, which looks some-what absurd to modern sensibilities and so heightens the impression of his pomposity.

Interestingly the use of this meme did not stop at the boundaries of the feminist community and those that shared their humour. In a Twitter discussion on the performance of naivety by US senior officials around why other nations would wish to enhance their defensive capabilities, one political commentator kept the foundational portrait but adapted the text: 'Adversaries are so hard to read'; 'I want to defeat your missile defences'; 'Such complex creatures'; 'Your missile defe . . . '; 'So mysterious' (Lewis on Twitter, 2021). The function of the meme was to suggest that, despite claims by US officials, the intentions of the US enemies were transparent and did not require any special interpretation. This evolution and redeployment of a meme into a new context is an everyday occurrence on social media, but its efficacy relies on audiences bringing an inherited knowledge from the meme's original usage to a new environment. To 'get the joke', the reader of this tweet would need to understand and reject the stereotype that women were 'complex' and 'mysterious', so that they could similarly reject such a claim on the part of the US State Department.

The evolution of humour here is suggestive of a shift in cultural ideas about women. The original meme relies on a common agreement, at least by a core audience, that men make claims to women's 'mysteriousness', that this is an untenable claim, and so it should be subject to ridicule through the meme format. Without some agreement as to the existence of the underlying sexism, the joke would fall flat. The new meme begins from the assumption that women's mysteriousness is ridiculous and uses that as a foundation for a commentary on foreign affairs. Within this new imagining of the world, the underlying sexism that provided a foundation for the original joke has lost its power – that women are not mysterious is now the status quo. It could then be suggested that this evolution in meme format marks a transition in social attitudes around women, where one stereotype has lost its cultural power. While this is not the same as saying that this attitude has entirely disappeared, not least given that social media users are their own distinctive community, it offers a hopeful clue as to the power of the meme to advance political causes and to change social attitudes. As Ringrose and Lawrence (2018) argue, being able to share in the 'in-joke' of the meme itself reinforces the sense that one is part of a select community and so invests individuals in the political project of that community. Moreover, as that group expands, so these ideas become a 'sustainable' part of popular culture.

Historical emotions provide modern audiences with an opportunity to build emotional communities through a shared political project, and to act as a site of contest over how the futures that we build and imagine for ourselves should look. If at times the historical emotions being mobilised are modern feelings projected backwards onto past bodies, the 'past' is not simply passive here. Rather, through their depictions of gendered feelings, paintings inspire social commentary and set boundaries around what can be imagined. Surprising survivals of female emotion, whether interpreted correctly or not, can offer legitimacy and authenticity to women's feelings of suffering today and so to their claims of injustice. Men holding gestures and positions that are read as overbearing or domineering become symbols of a long history of female suffering. Such emotion has political effects as it is circulated in the public sphere, as part of a genre that is now readily used to produce self and identity. Generations of feeling are marked not only in the transmission of historical emotions over time, but in their adaptation and reuse for new purposes.

7 Conclusion

The digital world offers a new site for emotional life, where rules of feeling are shaped by the nature of the environment, by the tools and technologies that contribute to emotional expression, and the emotional regimes that determine how such feeling will be received by audiences. Memes provide an important mechanism through which emotion is performed in the digital realm, particularly on fast-paced and quickly evolving social media sites. Historical art memes, where meme users deploy artworks, especially portraiture, to express a reaction to a particular circumstance or to build emotional communities, offer one example of a technology that is used to support emotional, digital lives, and one that deliberately plays with the relationship between past and present. This raises critical questions for historians, for scholars of digital media, and for emotionologists about why representations of past people provide such a fruitful resource for contemporary audiences in the expression of their own feelings. This Element has integrated insights from the history of emotions, art history, and digital media studies to offer an explanatory context for this phenomenon and to elucidate the function and performance of emotion in the digital realm.

All emotional expression speaks to the historicity and temporality of emotions, but historical art memes actively play with these ideas to express contemporary feeling, operating as a significant cultural currency for many online communities. Through the analysis of a selection of memes that remix classic artworks from the sixteenth to nineteenth centuries, this Element has demonstrated how incongruous facial expressions and lesser-known portraits offer a powerful and convenient proxy for the expression of emotions that are emerging, subversive, or challenging to express. The bored or impassive faces of historical women are taken out of context and redeployed to support the social, political, and sexual frustrations of women in the digital age. In a domain that leaves women vulnerable to various forms of male aggression, both on- and off-line, historical art memes provide a level of anonymity and security through which their voices can be heard, emotional communities built, and social attitudes changed. Through imagined acts of reciprocal violence, historical art memes can offer a space to fantasise about revenge or changing norms, using playful and humorous juxtapositions between text and image to provide opportunities for individuals to contest a violent status quo.

As this Element has shown, humour is critical to the meme, not least as it provides space to perform difficult-to-express feelings and to explore appropriate responses to novel social, political, and economic conditions. As anthropological studies suggest, an appreciation of the relationship between humour and liminality is important for demonstrating how social belonging and its boundaries are maintained (Turner, 1979). The concept of carnival, for example, highlights how tropes of debasement, ambiguity, and lower-body humour offer opportunities for people to enact cultural and political resistance (Stallybrass & White, 1986). Memes that deploy embodied emotional reactions, such as gasping in shock, crying in shame, or farting in public, are pitted against the disembodied omnipresence of the datafied digital realm, allowing people to express feelings that might otherwise disrupt what is expected of highly curated online personas.

In this setting the historical face used by the historical art meme might be considered as a mask, a tool, that like carnival, has a long and wide-ranging history in the expression of difficult emotions (Tonkin, 1979). The face of the historical art meme allows meme users to put a space between themselves and the message communicated, supporting political commentary and resistance to contemporary norms while limiting the vulnerability that such speech can generate. Through the historical art meme, digital media users use the face of an 'other' to communicate, an act that both aligns and distances individuals from the act of being 'seen' or emotionally exposed online. Moreover, putting distance between the meme and the user opens up a reading of emotional expression as spectacle, supporting alternative meanings and interpretations and offering the meme as a tool that can be deployed by other users for a variety of purposes. Within the framework of the historical art meme, emotional performances are given life beyond the individual and so support cultural life and its political effects.

Representations of emotion from the past are not passively deployed as part of modern performances of emotion but rely on the alterity of historical emotion. The liminality and part of the humour of such representations emerges due to the disjuncture between what is represented and its present use. People may deploy historical emotions as masks or props to support the production of contemporary emotional communities and their agendas, but past emotions are neither easily interpreted, nor straightforwardly captured within contemporary modes of feeling. Rather, their 'otherness' is critical to their efficacy, where surprising, confusing, or representationally complex components of historical art become part of what makes these artworks resonate for contemporary viewers. That memes are then used as extensions of the self – to express feelings or to build emotional communities – enables past feeling to have contemporary impact, where modern and online emotional cultures are not 'new' but produced in conversation with long histories of feeling and the expression of emotion on the bodies of shared ancestors.

If this use of historical art relies on the conceit of progress, that the meme utilises the 'foreignness' of the past to be effective opens up a variety of interpretations and possible futures. Past emotions allow modern audiences to grapple with complex and changing social conditions and to express difficult, subversive, or emerging emotions, whilst creating the conditions for their production. Historical art memes disclose the historical roots of new emotional experiences, which can be invoked by different actors to support diverse polit-ical agendas. As this Element has suggested, this history can be used product-ively in the present, to ground putatively new emotional experiences and offer security and safety in times of change.

Historical art memes offer insight into emotional life in the digital realm. The importance of emotion to the functioning of digital life, where engagement is expressed through likes and emoticons, and success relies on the capacity to express and elicit feeling, requires new forms of emotional performance and new understandings of the function of emotion in everyday life. Life online requires people to perform emotion to successfully navigate online spaces, placing them in a highly reflexive relationship to their own feelings. Emotion must be performed, but online spaces are fundamentally public and so require that the performance of emotion is curated for an external audience. In an 'always on' culture, individuals learn to deploy emotion strategically and safely, shaping their performances in relation to privacy settings and imagined viewers. This is not to suggest that performances of feeling are artificial or inauthentic, but acknowledges that the degrees of intimacy and vulnerability at stake between different actors are shaped by feeling rules for particular environments.

Notably within highly visual and curated online cultures, a person is most vulnerable, most intimate, in corporeal form, especially when the presentation of self is at its 'ugliest'. Here the politics of vulnerability in the digital realm actively plays with the absence of corporeality that, superficially at least, appears to be the central distinction between the on- and off-line world. Images of embodied emotion attempt to bridge that gap, whilst simultaneously reinforcing its existence. The faces of historical people act as reminders not only of an embodied past but its current absence. The capacity of people to negotiate the ambiguity of emotional expression as images of bodies move across time and context evidences a remarkable comfort with the multiplicity and temporality of emotional experience. If emotions are performed for online effects, and performances are inherently unstable and playful, then emotion cannot be held as universal or monolithic for online publics. Rather, histories of emotion – manifested in historical artworks – provide an opportunity to expand emotional repertoires and to negotiate a fast-paced, quickly evolving environment, where emotion is not simply a response to social conditions but active in their creation.

References

Adams, A. J. (2009). *Public Faces and Private Identities in Seventeenth-Century Holland: Portraiture and the Production of Community*, Santa Barbara: University of California.

Agamben, G. (2013). *Nymphs*, London: Seagull Books.

Aharoni, T. (2019). When high and pop culture (re)mix: An inquiry into the memetic transformations of artwork. *New Media & Society*, 21(10), 2283–304.

Ahmed, S. (2014). *The Cultural Politics of Emotion*, Edinburgh: Edinburgh University Press.

Ahmed, S. (2004). Affective economies. *Social Text*, 22(2), 117–39.

Akram, U., Ellis, J. G., Glhenda Cau, Frayer Hershaw, Ashlieen Rajenthran, Mollie Lowe, Carissa Trommelen & Jennifer Drabble (2021). Eye tracking and attentional bias for depressive internet memes in depression. *Experimental Brain Research*, 239(2), 575–81.

Al-Natour, R. (2020). The digital racist fellowship behind the anti-aboriginal internet memes. *Journal of Sociology*, 57(4), 780–805.

Bai, Q. Qi Dan, Zhe Mu, and Maokun Yang (2019). A systematic review of emoji: Current research and future perspectives. *Frontiers in Psychology*, 10 (2221). https://doi.org/10.3389/fpsyg.2019.02221.

Barad, K. (2003). Posthumanist performativity: Towards an understanding of how matter comes to matter. *Signs*, 28(3), 801–31.

Barad, K. M. (2007). *Meeting the Universe Halfway: Quantum Physics and the Entanglement of Matter and Meaning*, Durham: Duke University Press.

Barclay, K. (2021). Taking Bonnie Prince Charlie to heart: Children, emotion and rebellion. *Parergon*, 38(2), 157–85.

Barclay, K. (2020). *The History of Emotions: A Student Guide to Methods and Sources*, Basingstoke: Palgrave Macmillan.

Barclay, K. (2019a). *Men on Trial: Performing Emotion, Embodiment and Identity in Ireland, 1800–1845*, Manchester: Manchester University Press.

Barclay, K. (2019b). Falling in love with the dead. *Rethinking History*, 22(4), 459–73.

Barclay, K. (2017). New materialism and the new history of the emotions. *Emotions: History, Culture, Society*, 1(1), 161–83.

Barclay, K., Crozier-De Rosa, S., & Stearns, P., eds. (2020). *Sources for the History of Emotions: A Student Guide*, London: Routledge.

Barnes, D. G. (2017). Emotional debris in early modern letters. In S. Downes, S. Holloway & S. Randles, eds., *Feeling Things: Objects and Emotions Through History*, Oxford: Oxford University Press, pp. 114–32.

Beer, D. (2013). *Popular Culture and New Media: The Politics of Circulation*, London: Palgrave Macmillan.

Berlant, L. (2008). Thinking about feeling historical. *Emotion, Space and Society*, 1(1), 4–9.

Billig, M. (2005). *Laughter and Ridicule: Towards a Social Critique of Humour*, London: Sage.

Boddice, R. (2018). *The History of Emotions*, Manchester: Manchester University Press.

Bourdieu, P. (1986). *Distinction: A Social Critique of the Judgement of Taste*, London: Routledge.

Braidotti, R. (2019). *Posthuman Knowledge*, Cambridge: Polity Press.

Braidotti, R. (2013). *The Posthuman*, Cambridge: Polity Press.

Breheny, C. (2017). 'By any memes necessary': Exploring the intersectional politics of feminist memes on Instagram (Masters thesis, Uppsala University).

Bremmer, J. N., & Roodenburg, H. (1997). *A Cultural History of Humour: From Antiquity to the Present Day*, Cambridge: Polity Press.

Bristow, D., & Bown, A. (2019). *Post Memes: Seizing the Memes of Production*, Santa Barbara: Punctum Books.

Campbell, J. (2000). *The Hero with a Thousand Faces*, New York: Audio Renaissance.

Chagas, V., Freire, F., Rios, D., & Magalhães, D. (2019). Political memes and the politics of memes: A methodological proposal for content analysis of online political memes. *First Monday*, 24(2), https://doi.org/10.5210/fm.v24i2.7264.

Cheauré, E., & Nohejl, R. (2014). *Humour and Laughter in History: Transcultural Perspectives*, Bielefeld: Transcript Verlag.

Chonka, P. (2019). The empire tweets back? #HumanitarianStarWars and memetic self-critique in the aid industry. *Social Media + Society*, 5(4), https://doi.org/10.1177/2056305119888655.

Cover, R. (2015). *Digital Identities: Creating and Communicating the Online Self*, London: Academic Press.

D'Arcens, L. (2018). 'In remembrance of his persone': Transhistorical empathy and the Chaucerian face. In A. McKendry, M. Raine & H. Hickey, eds., *Contemporary Chaucer across the Centuries*, Manchester: Manchester University Press, pp. 201–17.

D'Arcens, L. (2014). *Comic Medievalism: Laughing at the Middle Ages*, Woodbridge: Boydell and Brewer.

D'Arcens, L. (2011). Laughing in the face of the past: Satire and nostalgia in medieval heritage tourism. *Postmedieval*, 2, 155–70.

D'Arcens, L., & Lynch, A. (2018). Feeling for the premodern. *Exemplaria*, 30(3), 183–90.

Davison, P. (2012). The language of internet memes, In M. Mandiberg, ed., *The Social Media Reader*, New York: New York University Press, pp. 120–34.

DeCook, J. R. (2018). Memes and symbolic violence: #Proudboys and the use of memes for propaganda and the construction of collective identity. *Learning, Media and Technology*, 43(4), 485–504.

de Groot, J. (2016). *Consuming History: Historians and Heritage in Contemporary Popular Culture*, London: Routledge.

de Groot, J. (2006). Empathy and enfranchisement: Popular histories. *Rethinking History*, 10(3), 391–413.

Deleuze, G., & Guattari, F. (1987). *A Thousand Plateaus: Capitalism and Schizophrenia*, trans. Brian Massumi, Minneapolis: University of Minnesota Press.

Dell, H. (2018). What to do with nostalgia in medieval and medievalism studies? *Emotions: History, Culture, Society*, 2(2), 274–91.

Department of History, Florida State University (20 May 2020). Meme Tuesday ... Facebook page, www.facebook.com/139850989436/photos/meme-tuesday-when-you-realize-your-zoom-session-started-20-min-ago-meme-credit-l/10158308585264437/.

Dolphijn, R., & van der Tuin, I., eds. (2012). *New Materialism: Interviews & Cartographies*, Ann Arbor: Open Humanities Press.

Douglas, N. (2014). It's supposed to look like shit: The internet ugly aesthetic. *Journal of Visual Culture*, 13(3), 314–39.

Downes, S., & Trigg, S. (2017). Facing up to the history of emotions. *Postmedieval*, 8, 3–11.

Eagleton, T. (1981). *Walter Benjamin, or, Towards a Revolutionary Criticism*, London: Verso Editions.

Ehrhart, M. J. (1999). Machaut's allegorical narratives and the Roman de la Rose. *Reading Medieval Studies*, XXV, 33–58.

Ellis, D., & Tucker, I. (2020). *Emotion in the Digital Age: Technologies, Data and Psychosocial Life*, London: Routledge.

Flecha Ortiz, J. A., Santos Corrada, M. A., Lopez, E., & Dones, V. (2020). Analysis of the use of memes as an exponent of collective coping during COVID-19 in Puerto Rico. *Media International Australia*, 178(1), 168–81.

Foreman, J. (2000). *Maskwork*, Cambridge: The Lutterworth Press.

Frosh, P., & Pinchevski, A. (2014). Media witnessing and the ripeness of time. *Cultural Studies*, 28(4), 594–610.

Fuchs, C. (2014). *Social Media: A Critical Introduction*, London: Sage.

Frevert, U. (2011). *Emotions in History – Lost and Found*, Budapest: Central European University Press.

Gal, N., Shifman, L., & Kampf, Z. (2016). 'It gets better': Internet memes and the construction of collective identity. *New Media & Society*, 18(8), 1698–714.

Gerbi, L. (2022). Romantic and socio-sexual scripts in eighteenth-century Britain (MPhil thesis, University of Adelaide).

Gerzic, M., & Norrie, A., eds. (2018). *From Medievalism to Early-Modernism: Adapting the English Past*, London: Routledge.

Goodman, D. (2005). Marriage calculations in the eighteenth century: Deconstructing the love vs. duty binary. *Proceedings of the Western Society for French History*, 33, http://hdl.handle.net/2027/spo.0642292.0033.009.

Grigore, G., & Molesworth, M. (2018), 'Pouring politics down our throats': Political CSR communication and consumer catharsis. In D. Crowther & S. Seifi, eds., *Redefining Corporate Social Responsibility*, Bingley: Emerald, pp. 71–86.

Grosz, E. (2011). *Becoming Undone: Darwinian Reflections on Life, Politics and Art*, Durham: Duke University Press.

Haraway, D. (2013). *Simians, Cyborgs and Women: The Reinvention of Nature*, New York: Routledge.

Haraway, D. J. (2003). *The Companion Species Manifesto: Dogs, People, and Significant Otherness*, Chicago: Prickly Paradigm.

Harlow, S., Rowlett, J. T., & Huse, L.-K. (2020). 'Kim Davis be like … ': A feminist critique of gender humor in online political memes. *Information, Communication & Society*, 23(7), 1057–73.

Hill, R. L., & Allen, K. (2021). 'Smash the patriarchy': The changing meanings and work of 'patriarchy' online. *Feminist Theory*, 22(2), 165–89.

Hochschild, A. (2012a). *The Managed Heart: Commercialisation of Human Feeling*, Berkeley: University of California Press.

Hochschild, A. (2012b). *The Outsourced Self: What Happens When We Pay Others to Live Our Lives for Us*, New York: Henry Holt.

Hotchin, J. (2017). Emotions and the ritual of a nun's coronation in late medieval Germany. In M. L. Bailey & K. Barclay, eds., *Emotion, Ritual and Power in Europe, 1200–1920*, Basingstoke: Palgrave, pp. 171–92.

Ignatow, G., & Robinson, L. (2017). Pierre Bourdieu: Theorizing the digital. *Information, Communication & Society*, 20(7), 950–66.

Isaac, M. (2021). Reddit is valued at more that $10 billion in latest funding round. *The New York Times*, 12 August. www.nytimes.com/2021/08/12/tech nology/reddit-new-funding.html.

Jane, E. (2017). 'Dude … stop the spread': Antagonism, agonism and #man-spreading on social media. *International Journal of Cultural Studies*, 20(5), 459–75.

Jenkins, H., Ito, M., & boyd, D.(2015). *Participatory Culture in a Networked Era: A Conversation on Youth, Learning, Commerce, and Politics*, Cambridge: Polity.

Jones, C. (2014). *The Smile Revolution in Eighteenth-Century Paris*, Oxford: Oxford University Press.

Kendon, L. (2004). *Gesture: Visible Action as Utterance*, Cambridge: Cambridge University Press.

Kessel, M., & Merziger, P. (2012). *The Politics of Humour: Laughter, Inclusion, and Exclusion in the Twentieth Century*, Toronto: University of Toronto Press.

Knobel, M., & Lankshear, C. (2014). Studying new literacies. *Journal of Adolescent & Adult Literacy*, 58(2), 97–101.

Koslofsky, C. (2014). Knowing skin in early modern Europe, c. 1450–1750. *History Compass*, 12(10), 794–806.

Leeker, M., Schipper, I., & Beyes, T. (2016). Performativity, performance studies and digital cultures. In M. Leeker, I. Schipper & T. Beyes, eds., *Performing the Digital: Performativity and Performance Studies in Digital Culture*, Bielefel: Transcript Verlag, pp. 9–18.

Lemmings, D., & Brooks A. (2014). The emotional turn in the humanities and social sciences. In D. Lemmings & A. Brooks, eds., *Emotions and Social Change: Historical and Sociological Perspectives*, London: Routledge, pp. 3–18.

Letherby, G., & Reynolds, G. (2005). *Train Tracks: Work, Play and Politics on the Railways*, Oxford: Berg.

Lewis, J. @ArmsControlWonk (21 September 2021). I find it very irritating . . . Twitter Page. https://twitter.com/armscontrolwonk/status/14403732703022 61252?s=21.

Li, K., & Biommaert, J. (2020). Please abuse me: Ludic-carnivalesque female masochism on Sina Weibo. *Gender and Language*, 14(1), 28–48.

Lovell, M. (1987). Reading eighteenth-century American family portraits: Social images and self-images. *Winterthur Portfolio*, 22, 243–26.

Lupton, D. (2020). Vital materialism and the thing-power of lively data. In D. Leahy, K. Fitzpatrick, & J. Wright, eds., *Social Theory and Health Education: Forging New Insights in Research*, London: Routledge, pp. 71–80.

Lupton, D. (2019). *Data Selves More-than-Human Perspectives*, Cambridge: Polity.

Lupton, D. (2018). Vitalities and visceralities: Alternative body/food politics in digital media. In M. Phillipov & K. Kirkwood, eds., *Alternative Food Politics: From the Margins to the Mainstream*, London: Routledge, pp. 151–68.

Lutzky, U., & Lawson, R. (2019). Gender politics and discourses of #mansplaining, #manspreading and #manterruption on Twitter. *Social Media & Society* 5(3), https://doi.org/10.1177/2056305119861807.

MacDonald, S. (2021). What do you (really) meme? Pandemic memes as social political repositories. *Leisure Sciences*, 43(1–2), 143–51.

Maddern, P. (2017). Reading faces: How did late medieval Europeans interpret emotions in faces? *Postmedieval*, 8, 12–34.

Makhortykh, M., & González Aguilar, J. M. (2020). Memory, politics and emotions: Internet memes and protests in Venezuela and Ukraine. *Continuum*, 34(3), 342–62.

Marini, M. Alessandro Ansani, Fabio Paglieri, Fausto Caruana & Marco Viola (2021). The impact of facemasks on emotion recognition, trust attribution and re-identification. *Scientific Reports*, 11, 5577. https://doi.org/10.1038/s41598-021-84806-5.

Matt, S. J., & Fernandez, L. (2019). *Bored, Lonely, Angry, Stupid: Changing Feelings about Technology from the Telegraph to Twitter*, Cambridge, MA: Harvard University Press.

McCosker, A., & Gerrard, Y. (2021). Hashtagging depression on Instagram: Towards a more inclusive mental health research methodology. *New Media & Society*, 23(7), 1899–919.

McCulloch, G. (2019). *Because Internet: Understanding the New Rules of Language*, New York: Riverhead Books.

McQuire, S., & Radywyl, N. (2010). From object to platform: Art, digital technology and time. *Time & Society*, 19(1), 5–27.

Meek, J. (2017). Risk! Pleasure! Affirmation! Navigating queer urban spaces in twentieth-century Scotland. In D. Simonton there are 8 authors., ed., *The Routledge Handbook of the History of Gender and Urban Experience*. London: Routledge, pp. 385–96.

Merrill, S., & Lindgren, S. (2021). Memes, brands and the politics of post-terror togetherness: Following the Manchester bee after the 2017 Manchester Arena bombing. *Information, Communication & Society*, 24(16), 2403–21.

Milner, R. M. (2016). *The World Made Meme: Public Conversations and Participatory Media*, Cambridge: The MIT Press.

Miltner, K. M. (2014). 'There's no place for lulz on LOLCats': The role of genre, gender, and group identity in the interpretation and enjoyment of an Internet meme. *First Monday*, 19(8), https://doi.org/10.5210/fm.v19i8.

Mitra, S. (2020). Memes, fears and suicide. *Australian & New Zealand Journal of Psychiatry*, 55(9), 927–27.

Moreno-Almeida, C. (2020). Memes as snapshots of participation: The role of digital amateur activists in authoritarian regimes. *New Media & Society*, 23(6), 1545–66.

Moyn, S. (2006). Empathy in history, empathizing with history. *History and Theory*, 45, 397–415.

Nagle, A. (2017). *Kill all Normies: Online Culture Wars from 4chan and Tumblr to Trump and the Alt-right*, Winchester: Zero Books.

Nash, A. (2017). Art imitates the digital. *Lumina*, 11(2), 110–25.

Nash, A. (2016). Affect, people, and digital social networks. In S. Y. Tettegah, ed., *Emotions, Technology, and Social Media: Communication of Feelings for, with, and through Digital Media*, London: Elsevier, pp. 3–21.

Nissenbaum, A., & Shifman, L. (2015). Internet memes as contested cultural capital: The case of 4chan's /b/ board. *New Media & Society*, 19(4), 483–501.

Nyffenegger, N. (2018). Blushing, paling, turning green: Hue and its metapoetic function in Troilus and Criseyde. In N. Nyffenegger & K. Rupp, eds., *Writing on Skin in the Age of Chaucer*, Berlin: De Gruyter, pp. 145–65.

Ott, B. L. Editor - Dana Cloud. (2017). Affect in critical studies. In *Oxford Research Encyclopaedia of Communication*, Oxford: Oxford University Press. https://doi.org/10.1093/acrefore/9780190228613.013.56.

Penney, J. (2020). 'It's so hard not to be funny in this situation': Memes and humor in U.S. youth online political expression. *Television & New Media*, 21 (8), 791–806.

Phillips, W., & Milner, R. M. (2017). *The Ambivalent Internet: Mischief, Oddity and Antagonism Online*, Cambridge: Polity.

Piaget, J. (2014). *Play, Dreams and Imitation in Childhood*, London: Routledge.

Plamper, J. (2015). *The History of Emotions: An Introduction*, Oxford: Oxford University Press.

Pollock, D. (1995). Masks and the semiotics of identity. *The Journal of the Royal Anthropological Institute*, 1(3), 581–97.

Raivio, O. (2016). Classical art memes as an affinity space: A faceted classification of an entertainment page (Pro Gradu thesis, University of Helsinki).

Reckwitz, A. (2012). Affective spaces: A praxeological outlook. *Rethinking History*, 16(2), 241–58.

Reddy, W. (2001). *The Navigation of Feeling: A Framework for the History of Emotions*, Cambridge: Cambridge University Press.

Rees, D. (2014). Down in the mouth: Faces of pain. In R. Boddice, ed., *Pain and Emotion in Modern History*, Basingstoke: Palgrave Macmillan, pp. 164–86.

Rentschler, C. A., & Thrift, S. C. (2015). Doing feminism in the network: Networked laughter and the 'Binders Full of Women' meme. *Feminist Themes*, 16(3), 329–59.

Retford, K. (2017). *The Conversation Piece: Making Modern Art in Eighteenth-Century Britain*, New Haven: Yale University Press.

Retford, K. (2006). *The Art of Domestic Life: Family Portraiture in Eighteenth-Century England*, New Haven: Yale University Press.

Ringrose, J., & Lawrence, E. (2018). Remixing misandry, manspreading, and dick pics: Networked feminist humour on Tumblr. *Feminist Media Studies*, 18(4), 686–704.

Rosenwein, B. (2015). *Generations of Feeling: A History of Emotions, 600–1700*, Cambridge: Cambridge University Press.

Rosenwein, B. (2011). *Emotional Communities in the Early Middle Ages*, Ithaca: Cornell University Press.

Roy, D. (2015). Masks and cultural contexts drama education and Anthropology. *International Journal of Sociology and Anthropology*, 7, 214–18.

Safra, L., Chevalier. C., Grézes, J., & Baumard, N. (2020). Tracking historical changes in trustworthiness using machine learning analyses of facial cues in paintings. *Nature Communications*, 11, 4728. https://doi.org/10.1038/s41467-020-18566-7.

Sandbye, M. (2014). Looking at the family photo album: A resumed theoretical discussion of why and now. *Journal of Aesthetics & Culture*, 6(1), 25419. https://doi.org/10.3402/jac.v6.25419.

Schama, S. (1987). *The Embarrassment of Riches: An Interpretation of Dutch Culture in the Golden Age*, New York: Alfred A. Kopf.

Schankweiler, K. (2020). Reaction images and metawitnessing. *Parallax*, 26 (3), 254–70.

Schankweiler, K., Straub, V., & Wendl, T. (2018). *Image Testimonies: Witnessing in Times of Social Media*, London: Routledge.

Scheer, M. (2012). Are emotions a kind of practice (and is that what makes them have a history)? A Bourdieuian approach to understanding emotion. *History and Theory*, 51(2), 190–220.

Shifman, L. (2014). *Memes in Digital Culture*, Cambridge, MA: The MIT Press.

Silvestri, L. E. (2021). Precarity, nihilism, and grace. *International Journal of Cultural Studies*, 24(2), 360–77.

Silvestri, L. E. (2018). Memeingful memories and the art of resistance. *New Media & Society*, 20(11), 3997–4016.

Sover, A. (2018). *The Languages of Humor: Verbal, Visual, and Physical Humor*, London: Bloomsbury Academic.

Stallybrass, P., & White, A. (1986). *The Politics and Poetics of Transgression*, New York: Cornell University Press.

Stearns, P., & Stearns, C. (1985). Emotionology: Clarifying the history of the emotions and emotional standards. *American Historical Review*, 90(4), 813–36.

Sutcliffe, A., Maerker A., & Sleight, S. (2018). *History, Memory and Public Life: The Past in the Present*, London: Routledge.

Tandoc, E. C., & Takahashi, B. (2016). Log in if you survived: Collective coping on social media in the aftermath of Typhoon Haiyan in the Philippines. *New Media & Society*, 19(11), 1778–93.

Tettegah, S. Y. (2016). *Emotions, Technology, and Social Media*, London: Elsevier.

Tonkin, E. (1979). Masks and powers. *Man*, 14(2), 237–48.

Turner, V. (1979). Frame, flow and reflection: Ritual and drama as public liminality. *Japanese Journal of Religious Studies*, 6(4), 465–99.

Wiggins, B. E. (2019). *The discursive power of memes in digital culture: ideology, semiotics, and intertextuality*. Routledge.

WikiVictorian @wikivictorian (7 September 2021). The Irritating Gentleman … Twitter Page. https://twitter.com/wikivictorian/status/1435013147740487681?s=21.

Wilkins, K. (2014). Valhallolz: Medievalist humor on the internet. *Postmedieval*, 5, 199–214.

Willenborg, J. P. (2019). To meme, or not to meme: Applying the theory of motivated information management to the provision of support after depressed individuals share suicidal memes (MA thesis, University of Wisconsin-Milwaukee,).

Williams, R. (2000). The business of memes: Memetic possibilities for marketing and management. *Management Decision*, 38(4), 272–9.

Zuboff, S. (2019). Surveillance capitalism and the challenge of collective action. *New Labor Forum*, 28(1), 10–29.

Acknowledgements

We would like to thank Bronwyn Reddan and Anna Cordner for their research assistance on this project.

Cambridge Elements ☰

Histories of Emotions and the Senses

Series Editors

Rob Boddice
Tampere University

Rob Boddice (PhD, FRHistS) is Senior Research Fellow at the Academy of Finland Centre of Excellence in the History of Experiences. He is the author/editor of 13 books, including *Knowing Pain: A History of Sensation, Emotion and Experience* (Polity Press, 2023), *Humane Professions: The Defence of Experimental Medicine, 1876–1914* (Cambridge University Press, 2021) and *A History of Feelings* (Reaktion, 2019).

Piroska Nagy
Université du Québec à Montréal (UQAM)

Piroska Nagy is Professor of Medieval History at the Université du Québec à Montréal (UQAM) and initiated the first research program in French on the history of emotions. She is the author or editor of 14 volumes, including *Le Don des larmes au Moyen Âge* (Albin Michel, 2000); *Medieval Sensibilities: A History of Emotions in the Middle Ages*, with Damien Boquet (Polity, 2018); and *Histoire des émotions collectives: Épistémologie, émergences, expériences*, with D. Boquet and L. Zanetti Domingues (Classiques Garnier, 2022).

Mark Smith
University of South Carolina.

Mark Smith (PhD, FRHistS) is Carolina Distinguished Professor of History and Director of the Institute for Southern Studies at the University of South Carolina. He is author or editor of over a dozen books and his work has been translated into Chinese, Korean, Danish, German, and Spanish. He has lectured in Europe, throughout the United States, Australia, and China and his work has been featured in the *New York Times*, the *London Times*, the *Washington Post*, and the *Wall Street Journal*. He serves on the US Commission for Civil Rights.

About the Series

Born of the emotional and sensory "turns," *Elements in Histories of Emotions and the Senses* move one of the fastest-growing interdisciplinary fields forward. The series is aimed at scholars across the humanities, social sciences, and life sciences, embracing insights from a diverse range of disciplines, from neuroscience to art history and economics. Chronologically and regionally broad, encompassing global, transnational, and deep history, it concerns such topics as affect theory, intersensoriality, embodiment, human-animal relations, and distributed cognition. The founding editor of the series was Jan Plamper.

Cambridge Elements ☰

Histories of Emotions and the Senses

Printed in the United States
by Baker & Taylor Publisher Services